Thirteen

ALSO BY Jonathan Cott

Stockhausen

City of Earthly Love

He Dreams What Is Going on Inside His Head

Charms

Forever Young

Pipers at the Gates of Dawn

Conversations with Glenn Gould

Dylan

The Search for Omm Sety

Visions and Voices

Wandering Ghost: The Odyssey of Lafcadio Hearn

Isis and Osiris: Exploring the Goddess Myth

DOUBLEDAY

New York

London

Toronto

Sydney

Auckland

Thirteen

13

A Journey

into

the Number

Jonathan Cott

Published by Doubleday
a division of Random House, Inc.

A hardcover edition of this book was
published in 1997 by Doubleday

Book Design by Marysarah Quinn
Original Jacket Design by Adriane Stark/Stark Design
Original Jacket Illustration: Mark Ryden

The Library of Congress has cataloged the
hardcover edition as:

Cott, Jonathan.
Thirteen : a journey into the number / Jonathan Cott
p. cm.
1. Thirteen (The number) I.Title.
GR933.C67   1996
133.3'.359 –dc20   96-16062
CIP

Hardcover Edition: ISBN: 0-385-47198-5
Paperback Edition: ISBN 978-0-385-51280-0

PRINTED IN THE UNITED STATES OF AMERICA

146484122

For Ann Druyan,

whose Birthday on June **13**

Makes 13 a Lucky Number

Acknowledgments

FOR THEIR SUGGESTIONS, advice, and help I am grateful to David Abba, Elizabeth Avedon, Janet Baldwin, Dawn Michelle Baude, Max Buten, Martha Crampton, Cathy Crane, Amy Dalton, Yolaine Destremau, Ernie Eban, Lisa Sigrid Frost, Elizabeth Garnsey, Richard Gere, Ellen Goldberg, Richard Grossinger, Julia Hillman, Robert Hoffstein, Lindy Hough, Betty Lundsted, Michele Napear, Peter Nilsson, John-Erik Omland, Murray Saltzman, R. Wayne Shoaf, Amy Sorrell, Ariel Spillsbury, Shirley Sun, Mark Swed, Kathi-Ann Tacy, Robert Thurman, Uma Thurman, Eliza Truitt, Aileen Ward, Elizabeth Whitney, Jody Winters, Hannah Wolski.

In beginning my investigation of the number 13, I got my bearings on the subject from two suggestive magazine articles—"*Triskaidekaphobia* Can Strike When You're Most Expecting It" by Paul Hoffman in *Smithsonian* (February 1987) and "Thirteen at Table" by Vincent Starrett in *Gourmet*

Acknowledgments

(November 1966)—and from the chapters "Why Is 13 Unlucky?" by Keith Ellis in *Number Power in Nature, Art, and Everyday Life* and "Lucky or Unlucky?" by Annemarie Schimmiel in *The Mystery of Numbers*.

Special thanks to my editor, Bruce Tracy, to my agent, Michael Carlisle, to Marysarah Quinn who designed the book, and to Mrs. Jacqueline Onassis and Scott Moyers who started me on the way.

Contents

1. Introduction **3**

2. Friday, January 13, 1995 **13**

3. Unlucky 13 **29**

4. Thirteen on 13 **35**

5. Friday, October 13, 1995 **131**

THIRTEEN: (interj) lunch counter . . . *A signal that the manager is nearby* (fr. the unluckiness of the number 13).
　—*The Dictionary of American Slang,* Edited by Robert L. Chapman

"Stand by, 13, we're looking at it."
　—NASA Control Center in Houston, Texas, acknowledging
　the explosion of an oxygen tank serving the command ship
　of the ill-fated 1970 Apollo 13 mission

THIRTEEN: 1. *luck* . . . originally a holy number, therefore numinous.
　—*Dictionary of Symbols and Imagery*
　by Ad De Vries

Thirteen

1.

Introduction

I T WAS A DINNER PARTY like any other, where one of the persons seated next to you inevitably asks, as William Wordsworth once inquired of the leech gatherer, "How is it that you live, and what is it you do?" In less resonant parlance, my interlocutor that evening wondered, "You're a writer? What do you write? How many books have you written? What are they about? Do they make any money? What are you working on now?"—the usual catechism to while away the appetizer.

In any case, one of those questions had got me thinking: How many books *had* I written? I counted them up in my mind. "Twelve," I replied. What was my next work? I didn't know, I said . . . but it would be my thirteenth, I thought to myself. I recalled the first sentence of George Orwell's *1984:* "It was a bright cold day in April and the clocks were striking thirteen." There was something disconcerting about that number.

I don't consider myself a superstitious person. I admit that I try to avoid walking under ladders or opening umbrellas indoors; and I knock on wood, literally or symbolically, and cross my fingers to wish someone good luck.

But that is as far as it goes. In principle, I agree with Spinoza's perspicacious comment that "men would never be superstitious, if they could govern all their circumstances by set rules, or if they were always favored by fortune: but being frequently driven into straits where rules are useless, and being often kept fluctuating pitiably between hope and fear by the uncertainty of fortune's greedily coveted favors, they are consequently, for the most part, very prone to credulity."

Thirteen, after all, is simply a prime number that succeeds 12 and precedes 14. Was it just cultural conditioning, then, that made me anxious about the number 13 and about Friday the 13th as well? "So have I heard," as Horatio says about the ghost of Hamlet's father, "and do in part believe it." But certainly I wasn't a hard-core triskaidekaphobe—someone suffering from a morbid fear of the number 13, like the poet Gabriele D'Annunzio who, throughout the year 1913, dated his correspondence "1912 + 1", or like the composer Arnold Schoenberg who, at the age of 76 (7 + 6 = 13), took to his bed, depressed, on Friday the 13th of July, 1951, and died thirteen minutes before midnight.

No doubt these are extreme cases. More generally, however, as we are informed by Paul Hoffman in *Smithsonian,* "as recently as 1978 it was estimated that triskaidekaphobia costs America a billion dollars a year in absenteeism, train and plane cancellations and reduced commerce on the thirteenth of the month." A public relations spokesperson for Continental Airlines told me, "Some people still don't like traveling on Friday the 13th. You can almost always get a ticket on Friday the 13th—unless you're going to Transylvania!" The main clock of the Geneva International Airport used to display the hours ". . . 12, 12a, 14 . . . ," and the number 13 was omitted from the arrival and departure gates. There is, moreover, no operating room numbered 13 at Johns Hopkins Hospital in Baltimore, Maryland, since, according to a hospital spokesperson, "patients have enough anxiety without seeing that number above the door as they are wheeled in." Obvi-

Old Hungarian Health Spell

When somebody is ill, and all the herbal medicines and the doctor's medicine seem to be no help to this person, perform this as a last try.

Lay the ill person naked in a beam of full moonshine. Have one basket filled with **13 fresh eggs** and another basket that is empty. Take one egg at a time and rub it on the person's skin slowly, touching all the crevices. When the entire egg surface is used, take the next fresh egg and place the used one in the empty basket. While you do this, say:

> By the power of Diana, by the power of Aradia,
> May all that is ill be absorbed into this egg.
> By the power of Queen Isis, so mote it be.

When all thirteen eggs are used, take a little water, bless it, put salt in it, bless it again, and sprinkle it around the corners of the sickroom, saying:

> The Goddess blesses her child. All is well now.
> Fresh new health will glow.

Dispose of the eggs in a living body of water, or bury them. Do not eat the eggs or you will get the illness.

ously, many hotels and apartment buildings still operate as if passing from the twelfth to the fourteenth floor on an elevator will make the thirteenth nonexistent.

Several hotel managers to whom I recently spoke, however, estimate that not more than ten percent of their hotel guests currently refuse to stay on the number-13 floors that do exist at places such as the Plaza or the Waldorf-Astoria in New York City. Recent surveys of both college students and adults report that superstitions such as walking under ladders, knocking on wood, and picking up pennies from the street for good luck are more prevalent today than fretting about the number 13.

Still, when I had been asked what my thirteenth book would be about, I was surprised to find myself thinking more about the sinistrous number than about a possible subject. To extirpate the incipient signs of triskaidekaphobia, I decided to telephone several friends and acquaintances to find out what they thought about the number 13.

"Thirteen is the number of a witches' coven!" exclaimed one person.

"Thirteen signifies completeness or infinity," a mystical friend told me. "It is a holy number and cannot be divided. There are twelve universes, and the thirteenth is God."

A Spanish friend recited a Spanish proverb: *"Martes trece ni te cases ni te embarques"* ("Don't get married or begin a trip on Tuesday the 13th").

"I don't like to admit it," a publishing friend told me, "but I never begin anything new on the 13th of the month. And I call in sick for work on Friday the 13th."

"Don't sleep thirteen in a bed," advised my aunt.

"For Miles Davis's thirteenth birthday," a jazz aficionado told me, "his parents gave him his first trumpet."

"When I was thirteen, I became a man," said a Jewish friend, remembering his bar mitzvah.

"Thirteen is the Death card in the Tarot deck," someone else informed me.

"Thirteen represents the completion of a cycle," said another person, "and going out of it through death or through liberation is the thirteenth step."

"When the speed of the wind reaches exactly thirteen miles per hour in Southern California," an acquaintance from San Diego revealed to me, "an organization here known as 'Call of the Wind' will beep its subscribers to notify them that the surf's up. I've heard of guys," my acquaintance continued, "who were all dressed up in suits and ties, driving to work, and when they heard the beep, they made a detour for the nearest beach, stripped down to their bathing suits, and caught a wave before heading back to the office."

"In my seventeen years of practice," asserted a clinical social worker at a center for anxiety and related disorders, "I've never seen anyone's life affected by fear of the number 13." (Obviously she didn't know about D'Annunzio and Schoenberg.) "A phobia is a mental illness, 'Friday the 13th' is not. If it's really so severe, the person probably has an obsessive-compulsive disorder." (But why not so frequently about numbers like 6 or 11 or 27?)

"I *never* sit down to eat at a table with twelve other people," an older acquaintance declared. "Thirteen at a table is just not done."

"People are spooked by anything today," a professor friend declared. "They don't want to court disaster so they stay away from the thirteenth floor, or whatever. Personally, I think we need a new Voltaire to set everyone straight."

Voltaire had little use for any kind of superstitions, numerical or otherwise. For him, one person's customs or beliefs

> **13 Help**
>
> **13,000 gallons** of Gatorade were dispensed at water stations by the New York Road Runners Club during the New York City Marathon on November 12, 1995.

were another person's superstitions. "A Frenchman traveling in Italy," he wrote in his *Philosophical Dictionary,* "finds almost everything superstitious, and is hardly wrong. The archbishop of Canterbury claims that the arch-bishop of Paris is superstitious; the Presbyterians levy the same reproach against his Grace of Canterbury, and are in their turn called superstitious by the Quakers, who are the most superstitious of men in the eyes of other Christians." As Gustav Jahoda remarks in *The Psychology of Superstition,* "One cannot divide the peoples of the world into the superstitious and the en-lightened, but only into those by and large more or less superstitious." The propensity toward superstition, said the Scottish philosopher David Hume, cannot be eradicated because it is an intrinsic part of our adaptive mecha-nisms of survival. But another Scotsman, Hugh Miller, saw it in a different light. To this nineteenth-century writer, superstitions were "the workings of that religion natural to the human heart."

It should not be surprising that numbers can be the basis of superstitious belief. The mathematician and philosopher Pythagoras, born in the sixth century B.C., believed that "numbers contain the secret of things." The Neo-platonic philosopher Plotinus asserted that "numbers exist before the ob-jects described by them; the variety of sense objects merely recalls to the soul the notion of number." And the twentieth-century architect Le Cor-busier stated: "Behind the wall, the gods play. They play with numbers of which the Universe is made up."

For Gnostics, Kabbalists, numerologists, and other mystics throughout the ages, numbers were a means of trying to understand, control, and ma-nipulate reality. They developed a mystique, character, and even sexual identity of their own (the Pythagoreans classified the odd numbers as mas-culine, the even numbers as feminine). They embodied the rhythms of our inner and outer lives. With them, as with the combination to a safe, you could lock and unlock the mysteries. And they contained mana.

There is no doubt that the number 13 has a special kind of power—almost always negative in our culture and consciousness. My investigation of 13 soon revealed to me, to a greater extent than I might have ever imagined, that it was a number that disturbed me. When I saw it coming, I stepped aside to let it pass by; when I came upon it, I headed the other way. So I decided to explore the many curious facets of this calumniated number to find out what taboos and revelations it concealed, and to turn my superstition into my thirteenth book.

2.

Friday,

January **13**,

1995

N Monday, January 9, 1995, I received a telephone call from Murray Saltzman, an insurance broker from Ardmore, Pennsylvania, just outside of Philadelphia, informing me that a meeting of the Philadelphia-based Friday the 13th Club, of which he was copresident, was going to take place in the city in four days, and that since one of the club's thirteen members was ill, might I be able to attend as an alternate? "Of course," I said. "Wonderful," said Murray. "Then we'll be thirteen for lunch. Join us at twelve-thirteen . . . and don't forget your black umbrella."

Philadelphia's Friday the 13th Club, a nonprofit organization, was founded in 1936 by Philip Klein, a local advertising executive and philanthropist. Klein thought superstitions were silly ("We're the only ones in the country who cheered when the first-class mail rate was raised to thirteen cents," he commented in 1978) and also wanted to get some publicity for himself and his company. He conceived of a club of thirteen friends and business associates—the choice of members was at his discretion—who would gather every Friday the 13th at different sites in and around Philadel-

The 13 Weather-Related Disasters Covered by Insurance Companies

1. Hurricane
2. Tornado
3. Flood/Flash flood
4. Lightning
5. Blizzard
6. Avalanche
7. Ice storm
8. Dust storm
9. Hailstorm
10. Forest fire
11. Tsunami (tidal wave)
12. Drought
13. Heat wave/Cold wave

(Information supplied by the National Climatic Data Center, Asheville, North Carolina, and the Reinsurance Association of America, Washington, D.C.)

phia, including the top of the Benjamin Franklin suspension bridge, the outdoor stalls of the Ninth Street food market, a temporarily closed entrance ramp to the Schuylkill Expressway, the Penn Historical Society, and the Philadelphia morgue. At a typical club meeting, the members ate breakfast or lunch (thirteen at a table) and then proceeded to, among other things, walk under ladders while holding open black umbrellas, spill salt, and break mirrors, all to the astonishment, horror, or amusement of any onlookers.

This particular Friday the 13th was to be celebrated at the Liberty Place rotunda on Chestnut Street. So I boarded an Amtrak train to Philadelphia from New York, which auspiciously departed from Penn Station on Gate 13. Two hours later I was wandering around the domed rotunda area of Liberty Place, with its encircling complex of upscale boutiques. On the open gallery above were about twenty eateries, including cajun, creole, and pasta restaurants, a deli, and the ubiquitous espresso bar. Local newspapers and radio and television stations routinely cover the club's meetings, and several cameramen and photographers were already hovering around a table that was being set up in the center of the rotunda between a grand piano and an enormous pot of fronds, providing the effect of a greenhouse and a salon. As at any typical club get-together, members greeted each other and caught up with each other's news since the previous Friday the 13th, which had occurred in May 1994.

Murray Saltzman introduced me to Max Buten, Philip Klein's nephew and recently retired from the paint and wallpaper business, who is the other copresident of the club. "Fifteen years ago," Max told me, "my uncle needed someone who could supply mirrors for the meetings. At the time, I was in the glass business, so I got the mirrors, and I've been doing it ever since. Before he died," explained Max, "Philip Klein asked if Murray and I would take over the club. We have a nice group of people—mostly businessmen and one woman, a former banker named Nikki Marx. We all have a sense of humor, and we don't believe in bad luck. Though one of our members once had a flat tire," Max confessed. "But nobody has left our ranks because something terrible has happened to him."

"Once, a woman at the Farmers' Market heard we were coming," Murray continued, "so she took holy water and spread it around her counter and was considering taking the day off. She didn't, and in fact she joined us in some of the fun, and when we were through with her, she was a convert and was no longer frightened by Friday the 13th."

I was next introduced to Arthur Klein, the sixty-year-old son of the founder, who

13 Bloody Sunday

On January 30, 1972 ("Bloody Sunday"), **13 unarmed civilians** were shot and killed in Belfast when British troops clashed with Roman Catholic demonstrators, causing retaliatory actions by guerrillas in Northern Ireland and demonstrations south of the border.

informed me that none of the original members of the club are living, and that the second generation, mostly in their fifties, sixties, and seventies—along with Arthur's thirty-year-old son Alexander—will continue to meet every Friday the 13th through the year 2000, at which time the club will self-destruct in accordance with the wishes of his father. The last session of the club will therefore take place on October 13, 2000.

I also met the oldest member of the group, Robert Haakenson, who has been coming to meetings for thirty-five years. A Ph.D. in communications and a former associate director of corporate public relations, Haakenson recalled his introduction to the club in 1960. "I had been invited to speak to the Topical Pharmaceutical Association of the Delaware Valley," he told me, "and the date fell on Friday the 13th. So the program chairman said, 'Come on, liven up the speech a little bit and let's get some Friday the 13th in it.' I'd read about the Friday the 13th Club, and I got in touch with Philip Klein who said to me—as Murray Saltzman did to you—that I should come to the next club meeting, which was that next Friday. At noon we met on an island in the middle of the Delaware River. We walked halfway across the bridge, and when we arrived at the spot, lunch was served. Afterwards we went through the rituals—walking under a ladder, opening black umbrellas, throwing salt over the left shoulder, and lighting 'three on a match,' which I'm sorry to say is a superstition that we no longer practice."

"What one is that?" I asked.

"That's from the days of the trenches during World War I, when matches were scarce. The doughboys would light a match, and if you lit two cigarettes on it, OK, but three cigarettes on a match and you were dead because it gave enemy snipers a chance to aim and shoot you. That superstition is gone since this is now a smoke-free club."

By noon, the thirteen participants in the day's events—including myself—had arrived. Someone brought in a ladder from a nearby boutique, opened it, and across the top of the bars attached a steel black cat with painted Day-Glo green eyes. Then, charily, I joined the twelve members of the club as they stood in a line, murmuring an inaudible conjuration to my-self—a bit of protective magic the other members would not have counte-nanced. And as two television cameras filmed the parlous but raucous pro-cession, we opened our black umbrellas, lowered our heads, folded the umbrellas just enough to allow us to pass through the ladder's portals, and received the applause of the crowd that was looking on from the floor above. The Magnificent 13 then shook hands and gathered around Alexander Klein, the club's youngest member and Philip Klein's grandson, who placed a seven-by-six-foot mirror in an enormous flat box on the floor, raised a ham-mer, and smashed it into smithereens, again to an enormous cheer.

Author "under the ladder" during the Friday the 13th Club festivities on January 13, 1995. *Photo by Murray Saltzman.*

Two young women approached me, and one said, "What you're doing is *very* bad luck."

"Are you very superstitious?" I asked her.

Her friend interjected, "*I* never pass a knife hand-to-hand. I set it down and then pick it up. And I wouldn't travel in an airplane today."

"I'm not as superstitious as Jennifer," said her friend. "But why tempt it?"

A long-haired, slightly glazed-looking guy who had overheard the conversation approached the young women and advised them to watch, as he planned to do, the *Friday the 13th* dismemberment films—Parts III, V, VII, and VIII—that he said were going to be shown for most of that night on cable television.

Meanwhile, the insouciant club members had sat down at the table in the rotunda, and after spilling salt they ate lunch, proposed toasts, and answered questions from bemused and inquisitive bystanders. As one made nervous by Friday the 13th, I myself was somewhat reassured to learn from one passing scholar that no year can have more than three Fridays the 13th (the next such year will be 1998), or fewer than one. The mathematician B. H. Brown, however, proved in a 1933 issue of the *American Mathematical Monthly* that the 13th is more likely to fall on a Friday than on any other day. Another such proof by S. R. Baxter, then a thirteen-year-old schoolboy at Eton, appeared in *The Mathematical Gazette* in 1969.

Later, a woman informed several of us that Friday the 13th was in ancient times a sacred and festive day celebrated by women before it was invalidated and condemned by the ancient patriarchy; thirteen, she said, was the number of lunar revolutions in a year, thus a feminine number, and Friday derived its name from Freyja, the Norse goddess of love and fertility, the Nordic Venus. Thus Friday the 13th, she concluded, should actually be devoted to that goddess. "The day has been given very bad press," she said. "You guys are just making fun of the superstition, but actually you should be organizing a celebration for the goddess of love!"

FRIDAY, THE THIRTEENTH CLUB

Meetings of the Club will be held as follows:

JANUARY
1939, 1950, 1956, 1961,
1967, 1978, 1984,
1989, 1995.

FEBRUARY
1942, 1948, 1953,
1959, 1970, 1976,
1981, 1987, 1998.

MARCH ✳
1936, 1942, 1953,
1959, 1964, 1970,
1981, 1987, 1992,
1998.

APRIL
1945, 1951, 1956,
1962, 1973, 1979,
1984, 1990.

MAY
1938, 1949, 1955,
1960, 1966, 1977,
1983, 1988, 1994.

JUNE
1941, 1947, 1952,
1958, 1969, 1975,
1980, 1986, 1997.

JULY
1945, 1951, 1956,
1962, 1973, 1979,
1984, 1990.

AUGUST
1937, 1943, 1948,
1954, 1965, 1971,
1976, 1982, 1993,
1999.

SEPTEMBER
1940, 1946, 1957,
1963, 1968, 1974,
1985, 1991, 1996.

✳✳ OCTOBER
1939, 1944, 1950,
1961, 1967, 1972,
1978, 1989, 1995, 2000.

NOVEMBER
1936, 1942, 1953, 1959,
1964, 1970, 1981,
1987, 1992, 1998.

DECEMBER
1940, 1946, 1957,
1963, 1968, 1974,
1985, 1991, 1996.

✳ FIRST MEETING, 1936.
✳✳ LAST MEETING, 2000.

To give the world a break
we all should be dead by
2001

Cat Lost for 13 Days Inside Airline

On June 30, 1994, Carol Ann Timmel, 26, was taking a flight on Tower Air from New York City to Los Angeles, where she hoped to begin an acting career. Accompanying her was her brown, beige, and white tabby cat named Tabitha, and her kitty sister, Pandora. Somehow, Tabitha escaped from her animal carrier case in transit.

During the next **13 days,** traps laid with fresh tuna and water were strategically placed throughout the B-747 aircraft in an attempt to lure Tabitha from her hiding spot. Crew and maintenance teams continually probed the carrier in the air and at each port of call (Miami, San Juan, Los Angeles) when the plane was on the ground. Members of the Animal Adoption League and the ASPCA, along with a psychic brought by the cat's owner and a team of rescue specialists armed with minicameras, joined Carol Ann Timmel on innumerable forays into the plane's interior. Thirteen days and thirty thousand miles after the initial flight, Tabitha was discovered on July 12. "The general opinion here," said Carol Caver, a professional animal rescuer who helped find the cat, "is that Tabitha had some emotional issues to work out with her owner, herself, and her destiny. She must have resolved some of them to allow herself to be rescued."

I thought I would try to get Murray Saltzman interested in this excellent suggestion. But everyone was leaving: table and ladder were being carted off, cameras were being dismantled, and the only thing I could ask Murray amid the bustle was where the club would meet on the following Friday the 13th (October 13, 1995).

"You know that we never meet at a place more than once," Murray told me.

"Why is that?" I asked.

"Because no one ever wants us back," he said bemusedly. "But we're working on getting permission to meet up at the Miquon Post Office."

"Why there?" I asked.

"Because it's the smallest suburban post office in the Philadelphia area," Murray said. "In fact, it's a one-man post office, the man working there is postmaster, clerk, and janitor . . . and we've found out that it's closing on October 13, 1995. We hope to print up thirteen 'Last Day Issue' envelopes for the club members, with the postmark stamped by the postmaster. What better way to celebrate the day!"

THE IDEA OF a Friday the 13th club, or of a club devoted to ridiculing all forms of triskaidekaphobia, is not a new one. It seems to have originated in New York City on January 13, 1882, when the thirteen members of the Thirteen Club gathered in room 13 of the Knickerbocker Cottage at 454 Sixth Avenue (4 + 5 + 4 = 13) from 8:13 P.M. until 1 A.M. (the thirteenth hour). The club's initiation fee was $1.13, monthly dues thirteen cents, a lifetime membership thirteen dollars. Members dined on the 13th of every month, toasted to the health of Hermes Trismegistus (the legendary hermeticist who was said to have been "the thirteenth son of a thirteenth mother"), spilt salt, walked under ladders, and broke mirrors.

Eventually branch clubs sprang up around the country, and the national membership supposedly reached thirteen hundred, including President Chester Arthur, P. T. Barnum, and Decius S. Wade, Chief Justice of Montana, who had the dubious distinction of changing the traditional date of hangings from Friday (Hangman's Day) to Thursday.

Inspired by the New York Thirteen Club, the London Thirteen Club was founded in 1890. In his memoir, *Confessions of a Caricaturist,* Harry Furniss, the well-known cartoonist for *Punch,* recalls presiding over a club dinner on January 13, 1894, in room 13 of the Holborn Restaurant. Members and guests wearing green ties sat thirteen each at thirteen tables. Knives and forks were crossed, saltcellars were coffin-shaped, a "dim, religious light" emanated from skull-shaped lamps, cross-eyed waiters served the food, and each diner wore in his buttonhole a small coffin with dangling skeleton and peacock's feathers.

One of the guests that evening was soon revealed to be an undertaker from Bloomsbury who, having heard of the club dinner and believing that some of the members were sure to be struck dead in the near future, decided to attend. He presented his business card to Harry Furniss who stood up, introduced him to the company, and invited him to make the rounds of the tables and take orders.

"I detest Humbug," Furniss once wrote, "and Superstition is but another name for Humbug." One of the absent invitees of the Thirteen Club dinner apparently did not share Furniss's unwavering sentiments. Mr. George R. Sims sent a letter to Furniss to explain his absence that evening:

MY DEAR SIR, At the last moment my courage fails me, and I return the dinner ticket you have so kindly sent me.

If I had only myself to think of, I would gladly come and defy the fates, and do all that the members are pleased to do except wear the green necktie suggested by my friend Mr. Sala (that would not suit my complexion).

But I have others to think of—dogs and cats and horses—who if anything happened to me would be alone in the world.

For their sakes I must not run the risks that a faithful carrying out of your programme implies.

Trusting that nothing very terrible will happen to any of you in after life,

Believe me,

Sincerely yours,

[signed] GEO. R. SIMS

Basic to all Thirteen Clubs is that their members sit thirteen to a table, defying a particularly durable superstition. In Grose's 1787 *Provincial Glossary,* we are told, "Notwithstanding . . . opinions in favor of odd numbers, the number thirteen is considered as extremely ominous; it being held that, when thirteen persons meet in a room, one of them will die within the year." An eighteenth-century issue of the *Spectator* of London reported, "On a sudden an old woman unluckily observed there were thirteen of us in company. This remark struck a panic terror into several who were present, insomuch that one or two of the Ladies were going to leave the room: but a friend of mine, taking notice that one of our female companions was big with child, affirmed there were fourteen in the room, and that, instead of portending one of the company should die, it plainly foretold one of them should be born."

Napoleon would not dine with thirteen at a table. Neither would Herbert Hoover or Franklin Delano Roosevelt, this superstition being one of the few things they had in common. In *F.D.R., My Boss,* Grace Tully writes, "On several occasions I received last-minute summonses to attend a lunch or dinner party because a belated default or a late addition had brought the guest list to thirteen. My first invitation to a Cuff Links dinner, held annually on the President's birthday, came about in 1932 when with-

So What Is the Connection Between Number 13 and O. J. Simpson?

O. J. Simpson and Nicole Simpson were officially divorced on **July 13, 1993**. Nicole Simpson and Ronald Goldman each had **13 letters** in their names. Their dead bodies were discovered in Brentwood on **June 13, 1995**, at **12:13 P.M.**

drawal of one of the guests left a party of thirteen. I was an annual fixture after that."

To solve the long-term problems of its many superstitious diners, including Sir Winston Churchill whose private club regularly convened there, London's Savoy Hotel in 1926 commissioned the sculptor Basil Ionides to design a three-foot-high cat, which he carved from a single piece of plane tree. Christened Kaspar, he now lives on a high shelf in the Pinafore Room with his back to a mirror, and he is only removed if a party of thirteen is dining at the Savoy. He is then placed on the fourteenth chair with a napkin tied around his neck and is treated, in the words of a Savoy Hotel press release, "as a bona fide guest, the place settings before him changed as he is served each course of the meal."

When a wooden placebo like Kaspar isn't readily at hand, children are often called upon to perform a similar service. In her autobiography, *Haply May I Remember,* Cynthia Asquith recalls family parties at her grandmother's home in Wiltshire, where she was occasionally kept up at night to make a fourteenth at dinner. ("After the soup and fish," Cynthia Asquith wrote, "I was supposed to leave, and it was tantalizing to miss my dessert.")

Often a hostess facing the calamity of thirteen for dinner has been known to seat eleven people at one table and two at a smaller one (the "kindergarten table") a few inches away. Until recently in France, one was able at the last moment to telephone an agency and hire a fourteenth dinner guest called a *quatorzième*. The journalist Vincent Starrett tells the story of one of these professional diners who confessed the secret of what he did to an inquisitive woman sitting next to him at a Parisian dinner party. Soon after this introduction, the couple was married.

The most frequent explanation of the superstition that sitting thirteen at a dinner table may prove unlucky or fatal is that it summons up the ominous memory of the story of Jesus and his twelve apostles at the Last Supper: "Jesus answered them, Have I not chosen you twelve, and one of you is a devil? He spake of Judas Iscariot . . . for he it was that should betray him, being one of the twelve" (John 6:70–71).

In one version of the superstition it is said that whoever rises first from the table runs the greatest risk; in another that the last of the thirteen to take a seat will be doomed. In order to avoid the first danger, a hostess in Shropshire in 1883 used to urge her table of thirteen guests to rise carefully from their seats at the same moment. And at a dinner party described by C. Baron-Wilson in 1839, the hostess, a Miss Mellon, "always gave the last comer an equal chance with the rest for life. . . . She used to rise and say, 'I will not have any friend of mine sit down as the thirteenth; you must all rise, and we will then sit down together.' "

Those who have failed to observe such precautions have recorded many dire tales. Dining at the Savoy in 1898, for example, the South African mining magnate Woolf Joel gave a dinner party for fourteen. One guest canceled at the last minute. Joel left the table first. A few weeks later he was shot dead in his office in Johannesburg. And at one of James McNeill Whistler's breakfasts in London, thirteen guests sat down. It was reported that "there were two Miss C's, the younger of whom died within a week of the breakfast; and an elderly gentleman, when he heard of it at his club, said 'God bless my soul!,' had a stroke and died too."

Henrik Ibsen begins his play *The Wild Duck* with a dinner party for thirteen, and ends it with the suicide of a young girl, drawing not only on the story of the Last Supper but also, perhaps, on a much earlier Scandinavian myth in which the trickster god Loki crashes a banquet for twelve at Valhalla, culminating in the death of the heroic god Balder. Conversely, fairy tales often remind us what deleterious effects can occur when a "thirteenth" is unwittingly *not* invited. In the Brothers Grimm's "Briar Rose," for instance, the thirteenth Wise Woman of the kingdom, overlooked because the king has only twelve gold dinner plates, manifests herself as the Wicked Fairy and puts a curse on the baby princess that results in her long sleep but ultimate joyful awakening.

In such mysterious ways does 13 bring forth both its woes and triumphs. In 1873, Mr. N. Brandt wrote to Harry Furniss of the London Thirteen Club:

SIR, I see you are going to have an anniversary dinner on the 13th of this month, and I take the liberty to send you the following:

In 1873, March 20th, I left Liverpool in the steamship *Atlantic,* then bound for New York. On the 13th day, the 1st of April, we went on the rocks near Halifax, Nova Scotia. Out of nearly 1,000 human beings, 580 were frozen to death or drowned.

The first day out from Liverpool some ladies at my table discovered that we were thirteen, and in their consternation requested their gentleman-companion to move to another table. Out of the entire thirteen, I was the only one that was saved. I was asked at the time if I did not believe in the unlucky number thirteen. I told them I did not. In this case the believers were all lost and the unbeliever saved. . . .

At the North-Western Hotel, in Liverpool, there can be found thirteen names in the book of passengers that left in the *Atlantic* on the 20th of March, 1873, for New York; amongst them my own. Every one of those passengers except myself were lost.

I am very truly,

[signed] N. BRANDT

3.

Unlucky

13

HE NOVELIST TOM ROBBINS once asserted that he never got out of bed in the morning until he turned on the radio and heard someone mention the number 23—his favorite number. "You'd be surprised how often that number comes up," said Robbins. On the radio, of course, someone is always announcing the time, the temperature, the year a rock song was first released, the number of days before Christmas. But would the novelist ever get out of bed if he waited for the number 181, say, to be spoken? The point, however, may be that if one fixes one's attention on something, one's "number" is bound to come up.

I am writing this on June 26 (13 × 2), 1995. I am now glancing at today's edition of the *New York Times,* and on page B3 I find the headline MAN RECALLS SUDDEN DROP ON CONEY ISLAND RIDE THAT HURT 13, and then, on the same page, an article about a reclusive Upper East Side woman who has been killed in her apartment building. The victim's cousin, it is reported, "who hadn't seen the victim for 13 years, recognized her photograph in the newspapers and went to the morgue to identify her body." In these instances, I'm certain that if only twelve people had been hurt or only twelve

The Clock People and the Number 13
(from *Even Cowgirls Get the Blues*
by Tom Robbins)

In *Even Cowgirls Get the Blues,* Tom Robbins writes of the Clock People—
a gathering of Native Americans from various tribes—who, after the
1906 San Francisco earthquake, migrated into the Sierras "where, in a
period of **13 full moons,** they generated the stalk of a new culture,"
keeping **26 (13 x 2) hour days:**

The Clock People, as we now know them, divided themselves into
thirteen families, not necessarily along tribal lines. (What is the
numerical significance of the Clock People's taking thirteen months
to structure their ritual, then separating into thirteen families? Well,
briefly, they consider thirteen a more natural number than twelve.
To the Babylonians, thirteen was unlucky. That is why, when they
invented astrology, they willfully overlooked a major constellation,
erroneously assigning to the zodiac only twelve houses. The Clock
People knew nothing of Babylonian superstition, but they knew the
stars, and it was partly in an effort to override the unnatural twelve-
mindedness of Western culture that they chose to give thirteen its
due.) To each family was assigned the responsibility for one section of
the Great Burrow. Each family knows one section inch by inch, but is
completely ignorant of the other twelve sections. So no one family
nor individual knows the Way. The Way, of course, being the true path
that takes one through the Great Burrow maze to the clockworks.
Moreover, it is not possible for the families to compile a map of the
Way, for each family holds as a sacred secret its knowledge of its
burrow or section of the Way.

years of absence had elapsed, the significance of the stories would have been the same. If twelve or fourteen people sit at a dinner table—especially twelve or fourteen older people—there is a good chance that something unpleasant or distressing may shortly occur to one of them, and certainly within a year.

The *British Medical Journal* recently released a study evaluating the number of hospitalizations on Fridays the 13th. It found that falls, animal bites, poisonings, and car accidents were more numerous on that date. And the journal found it impossible to say whether the day itself was unlucky or that the psychological weight attached to that date made people more susceptible to those accidents. Negative prophecies, after all, are always goads for dire consequences.

Still, in spite of reason and common sense, the number 13 does not easily relinquish its sinistrous powers, both subconscious and unconscious, that easily. In the European tradition, 13 has been a number of necromancy: It is the diviner's traditional card of death, and people were said to animate corpses with thirteen needles. It is, most famously, the traditional number of the coven of witches—twelve women and the Horned God, who was later perverted by the Church into the image of the devil—whose symbol was the pentacle overlapped by a triangle, giving a total of thirteen sides. And Robert Graves suggests that the thirteen-month calendar that survived among European peasants for more than a millennium after the official adoption of the Gregorian calendar, required a human sacrifice in the thirteenth month, and that the number henceforth gained its baleful reputation.

The number 12, on the other hand—and it happens to be my favorite number—is often said to symbolize totality, perfection, a completion: the twelve signs of the zodiac, the twelve gods of Olympus, the twelve tribes of Israel, the twelve Imams, the twelve Gates of Heaven, the twelve months of the year, the twelve hours of the day, the twelve-tone musical scale, the twelve subatomic building blocks—quarks and leptons—now believed to constitute all the material world. Into these systems, the number 13 brings a kind of instability, an element of intrusiveness, confusion, uncanniness, and disorder.

In the Babylonian calendar, for instance, the lunar year consisted of 354 days, and after a number of years a thirteenth month had to be intercalated in order to accommodate it to the solar year; the Babylonians called this month "Lord of distress" or "Lord of oppression." (Professor Aileen Ward wittily suggests that it was called this "because the people probably had to work an extra month with no pay.") And in our own times, an extra month was added in August 1995 to the Chinese lunar calendar to attune it to the solar calendar. Chinese tradition maintains that when the double month falls in August, which it does every nineteen years, tragedy will follow. During the double August in 1976, an earthquake in Tangshan killed 240,000 people. Floods and droughts devastated the country, a meteorite struck, and Chairman Mao Ze-dung died. In 1995, however, although there were reports of raining frogs, floods, and several earthquakes, the valetudinarian Communist Party leader Deng Xiaoping somehow survived his ninety-first birthday.

As Professor Annemarie Schimmel states, "When a German says, '*Jetzt schlägt's Dreizehn*' (Now the clock is striking 13), it means that the closed circle has been transgressed and 'too much is too much!' " So I was surprised that when I made my first telephone call to a therapist and psychic in New York City to ask her about the number 13, she immediately said, "What a lucky number!" It was in this spirit, then, that I began my pilgrimage into the realm of 13, searching for thirteen people whose lives the number 13 had touched.

4.

Thirteen

on

13

IN THE MOST LITERAL SENSE, no one is touched more by the number 13 than the person who has the number tattooed on his or her body. Michael Malone, who tattoos between twenty and thirty 13's on customers every year, is the owner of the China Sea Tattoo shop in the heart of Chinatown in Old Honolulu. He bought the shop from his mentor, Sailor Jerry Collins, a legendary American tattooer who died in 1973. Born in 1942, Malone remembers putting a tattoo of a spider on himself when he was thirteen years old and then, at seventeen, tattooing a champagne glass on one of his friends, using a tattooing machine.

"When I started tattooing in the sixties," Malone told me, "the young people were asking for very cautious stuff—rainbows and unicorns. In the early seventies, however, I saw a lot of soldiers who were coming to Honolulu from Vietnam, and they had seen death and didn't have the idea that a lot of young people do that they're immortal, so they would go for more radical tattoos. Instead of getting a safe little rosebud on their hip, those guys were asking for big pinups on their arms, always bigger and crazier designs.

The Orient and the Number 13

In the Mo system of Tibetan divination, **the number 13** is said to belong to Penden Lhamo, the Tibetan form of the Buddhist goddess Sri Devi, the fierce protectress of the Dalai Lama and the Tibetan state. In this system of divination, three dice are thrown, which can result in numbers from 3 to 18. The number 12 is the unluckiest, the number 13 the most favorable.

There are said to be **13 stages to Buddhahood** consisting of ten bodhisattva stages and three additional pre-Buddhist stages.

"When the Vietnam War was over, you found that tattooing slid back so that we were doing a lot of rainbows and unicorns again. But now in the nineties, the real radicalism has returned, and I wonder whether it doesn't have something to do with the urban areas turning into free fire zones. Certainly it's got to do with the population growing so quickly and people needing to scream louder to be heard, so kids are poking rings through their noses and tattooing themselves all up. Lots of tattoos and in gigantic proportions. Recently I saw a girl who had two giant daggers tattooed from the top of her legs down to her ankles. That's radical."

"What style of tattoos are people interested in today?" I asked.

"Today," said Malone, "there's a movement back to old traditional-looking tattoos like those from the forties and fifties—big pinups, big eagles, patriotic-looking stuff. Another group is getting kind of tribal-looking designs based on art from Polynesia or Borneo, the way the Dayak headhunters got tattooed. There's also a movement now of biomechanical stuff that looks partly organic, partly machinelike. I don't find it very attractive, but there are people who admire that. But

Tattoo designs ' Michael Malone.

Tattoo designs © *Michael Malone.*

there's also an increasing interest in images like hearts, dice, horseshoes, daggers, Lady Luck, and rabbits' feet. I think this kind of classic imagery will get increasingly popular in the next five years."

"What about the number 13 design?" I asked.

"The 13 design is also very popular at the moment—the cat standing on the 13, for instance. In this society," said Malone, "13 is considered an unlucky number—you're taught that from the time you're a little kid—but in the tattoo business you find people who think it's lucky. It's always been a number that's appeared in tattoos—I have pictures of old tattoo designs that go back to the twenties, and the number 13 is prominent, and it's been just as prominent in European tattooing as it has here.

"It feels like a magic number, so people have toyed with it over the years. I know that when I design stuff with 13's, I don't have a mystical thing about the number, it doesn't scare me, I'm not afraid of it. (Personally, I've always shied away from the number 37; I wouldn't tattoo myself with that, not even for the fun of it.) And then there's the 13/marijuana connection. *M* is the thirteenth letter of the alphabet and it also stands for marijuana. That connection is big with Chicano gangs, which have existed since the thirties and forties, and they've always messed with 13 as a marijuana number.

"The number 13 is beautiful looking," said Malone. "It has a nice shape, more than the number 20, say. The 3 looks like an *Om*. In the *Om* there's a slash across the top and the 3 sits upright—a single flash above a stylized 3. You just move the line from the left side of the 3 and lay it on its side over the 3's head . . . and that's *Om*.

"I've had customers who bring in a prayer rug to sit on when they're being tattooed. But I'm not ritualistic about the process of tattooing. When I'm tattooing I'm performing my craft. You only get one shot at it, there's no eraser, you have to go in there, get your mind right, go after it, and do it. And to do it well you have to give it all your attention, but you can't worry about it. It has a spiritual aspect to it, but anyone dealing with any craft hooks into that.

"Tattooing is older than painting and drawing. Someone a long time ago poked himself with a burnt stick and noticed that it left a mark . . . and they were off! The Egyptian mummies had tattoos on them, the frozen Ice Age man in Austria had tattoos on him, and so do the mummified Scythians they've been finding in Siberia, one with a large elk tattooed across his back and chest. It's a shamanistic thing that goes all the way back."

. . .

The 13 House

In 1884, Sarah L. Winchester, the Winchester Rifle heiress, began construction of her lifelong obsession, the 160-room Winchester Mystery House in San Jose, California. Mrs. Winchester, who had lived in New Haven, Connecticut, was deeply upset by the death of her husband and daughter (he from pulmonary tuberculosis, she from marasmus one month after her birth), and she consulted a medium. Supposedly the medium explained that the spirits of all those who had been killed by the rifles her family manufactured had sought their revenge by taking the lives of her loved ones. Furthermore, these spirits had placed a curse on her and would haunt her forever. But the medium also stated that she could escape the curse by moving west, buying a house, and continually building on it as the spirits directed. In this way, she could escape them and perhaps find the key to eternal life.

One of the most extraordinary features of the house is the role that the number 13 plays in it. A partial list of the 13's in the house include:

13 cement blocks in the Carriage Entrance Hall
13 blue and amber stones in the spiderweb window
13 bathrooms
13 panels in the wall by the 13th bathroom
13 windows in the 13th bathroom
13 steps into the 13th bathroom
13 windows and doors in the old sewing room
13 hooks in the Seance Room
13 Ever-Flow drain holes in the Italian sink
13 rails by the spy hole in the South Conservatory
13 steps on the last flight to the fourth floor
13 ceiling panels in the Entrance Hallway
13 subpanels in the ballroom ceiling panels
13 glass cupolas in the greenhouse
13 holes in the drain-hole cover
13 gas jets on the Ballroom Chandelier
13 stones in the Oriental Bedroom windows
13 squares on each side of the Otis Electric Elevator

On April 13, 1984, the Winchester Mystery House officially celebrated one hundred years of Mystery, with the help of the Mountain Charlie Chapter No. 1850 of E Clampus Vitus, by unveiling a special 100th Anniversary Plaque commemorating Sarah Winchester and the Winchester Mystery House for "100 Years of Mystery." At **1300 hours** (1 P.M.), the bell in Mrs. Winchester's bell tower was rung **13 times;** and at the conclusion of the celebration, **1,300 balloons** were released into the air.

There are **13 parts to Sarah Winchester's will;** her signature appears in it **13 times.**

OF ALL THE ARTS, music is most connected to numbers. Pythagoras called music "an Arithmetic, a science of true numbers"; and one can indeed say that music is numbers in sound. Number mysticism is at the root of many composers' art. In the Middle Ages, there is often an identification between the notion of "perfection" and triple rhythm because of the latter's association with the Trinity. In the *Credo* to J. S. Bach's B Minor Mass, the composer presents forty-three entries of the plainsong melody because that number corresponds to the numerical value of the word *credo*. The name "Bach" itself is numerically equivalent to the number 14 (and "J. S. Bach" to its retrograde number, 41), and both numbers play a pervasive role in his compositions.

One could, of course, enumerate countless instances throughout the centuries of the alliance between music and numbers. One would think, however, that with the existence of the all-embracing twelve-tone scale, the number 13 would have a difficult time making its presence felt. In his book *The Magic Numbers of Dr. Matrix,* however, the mathematician Martin Gardner takes the case of Richard Wagner and points out that there are thirteen letters in Wagner's name. He was born in 1813, and $1 + 8 + 1 + 3 = 13$. Wagner composed thirteen major works. *Tannhäuser* was completed on April 13, 1845, and first performed on March 13, 1861. He finished *Parsifal* on January 13, 1882. *Die Walküre* was first performed in 1870 on June 26 ($13 \times 2 = 26$). *Lohengrin* was completed in 1848, but Wagner did not hear it played until 1861, exactly thirteen years later. He died on February 13, 1883. ("Note that the first and last digits of this year also form 13," writes Gardner.) Although all of this might seem inconsequential, coincidental, and anecdotal at best, Gardner's alter ego "Dr. Matrix" states, "Important dates are never accidental."

A more curious musical story touching on the number 13 concerns the late American composer John Cage. Cage's father, John Milton Cage, was an inventor who, in 1912, the same year as his son's birth, designed a submarine that broke the world's record for remaining underwater—though it never succeeded commercially because it left air bubbles on the ocean's surface. Shortly after the submarine's initial descent, the inventor took it down again—an "experimental trip," he called it—on a Friday the 13th with a crew of thirteen and stayed underwater for thirteen hours.

Eighty years later, three months before his death in 1992, John Cage the composer completed his final musical work, a piece that he called *Thirteen*. It was one of a series of some fifty so-called Number Pieces that Cage worked on during his last years, whose titles depended on the number of players who performed them. *Thirteen* was commissioned by the German conductor Manfred Reichert for his new music group Ensemble 13, named for the thirteen string musicians who originally comprised the ensemble. This slow, meditative piece, which Cage instructed should last precisely thirty minutes, was given its premiere in Gütersloh in 1993 and has since been recorded. In the words of Cage's biographer, Mark Swed, "It is a music that is not unlike being underwater. You know where you are, your environment is consistent and contained; yet all is strange and slightly hallucinatory. . . . Cage's final, very aqueous piece is also an experiment. But in this case, it is a descent into a sonic realm not simply to prove that one can remain there. It is to explore."

It is perhaps more than coincidental, and certainly incongruous, that John Cage studied in the late 1930s with Arnold Schoenberg. Cage himself embraced what he called "an absence of musical law with regard to coexistence and multiplicity"; Schoenberg insisted on a rigorous control over the various levels of musical composition. Cage's use of numbers derived from the Chinese *I Ching,* Schoenberg's from the Western numerological tradition; his astonishing obsession with numbers has recently been uncovered and examined by Colin C. Sterne in his book *Arnold Schoenberg: The Composer as Numerologist,* which coincidentally contains a foreword by John Cage.

"It is not superstition, it is belief," said Schoenberg about his acceptance

How the World Almost Came to an End . . . in 13 Steps

The thirteen days in October 1962 that witnessed the confrontation between the United States and the U.S.S.R. over the Cuban Missile Crisis brought the world, as Robert F. Kennedy wrote in his book *Thirteen Days*, "to the abyss of nuclear destruction and the end of mankind. From [Tuesday morning, October 16, 1962] in President Kennedy's office until Sunday morning, October 28, that was my life—and for Americans and Russians, for the whole world, it was their life as well."

In an afterword to *Thirteen Days*, Richard E. Neustadt and Graham T. Allison ask, "How could nuclear war have emerged from this crisis?" And they summarize what happened during those thirteen days in the form of a scenario and then spell out one of the paths that could have led to war: **thirteen steps** in all.

1. The Soviet Union puts missiles in Cuba clandestinely (September 6, 1962).

2. U.S. U-2 flight discovers Soviet missiles (October 14, 1962).

3. President Kennedy initiates a public confrontation by announcing to the world the Soviet action, demanding Soviet withdrawal of the missiles, ordering a U.S. quarantine of Soviet weapon shipments to Cuba, putting U.S. strategic forces on full alert, and warning the Soviet Union that any missile launched from Cuba would be regarded as a Soviet missile and met with a full retaliatory response (October 22).

4. Khrushchev orders Soviet strategic forces to full alert and threatens to sink U.S. ships if they interfere with Soviet ships en route to Cuba (October 24).

5. Soviet ships stop short of the U.S. quarantine line (October 25).

6. Khrushchev letter offers withdrawal of Soviet missiles in return for U.S. noninvasion pledge (October 26), followed by a second Khrushchev letter demanding U.S. withdrawal of Turkish missiles for Soviet withdrawal of Cuban missiles (October 27).

7. Khrushchev announces withdrawal of the missiles (October 28).

Perhaps the most obvious scenario by which nuclear war might have emerged from the sequence follows the actual course of events through step seven, but then proceeds:

8. Khrushchev reiterates that any attack on Soviet missiles and personnel in Cuba will be met with a full Soviet retaliatory response (October 28).

9. U.S. "surgical" air strike against Soviet missiles (destroying all operational ballistic missiles and killing a limited number of Soviet personnel) (October 30).

10. Soviet medium-range ballistic missiles attack U.S. missiles in Turkey (destroying all ballistic missiles and killing a small number of Americans) (October 31).

11. In accord with obligations under the NATO treaty, U.S. medium-range missiles in Europe attack bases in the Soviet Union from which missiles that attacked the Turkish bases were launched (October 31).

12. Soviet Union, fearing additional U.S. attacks on its limited number of ICBMs, attacks the U.S. (November 1).

13. U.S. ICBMs attack the Soviet Union (November 1).

of the infallibility and inevitability of the power of numbers. Born on September 13, 1874, the composer was an unmitigated triskaidekaphobe in both his musical and private lives. "All things considered," he wrote to the composer Anton Webern, "I'll be happy when this ominous 1926 year is over. Then it will be the 52nd year of my birth (4 × 13) and the 26th year after 1900 (2 × 13), which is 2 × 13 years after my birth year [1874], which is equal to 1874 + 26 + 26." Schoenberg's musical inspiration often flagged at measures or pages on his score numbered 13 or its multiples. His numbering of measures in his compositions invariably used the sequence 12, 12a, 14. In his opera *Moses und Aron,* he insisted on spelling the name Aaron with one "a" in order to avoid a title with thirteen letters.

On September 13, 1939, Schoenberg realized that his age would be 5 × 13; moreover, the final two digits of that year, 39, were 3 × 13. The composer and astrologer Dane Rudhyar cast Schoenberg's horoscope; Rudhyar reported back that the last few months of 1939 would prove difficult for Schoenberg, but if he survived them he would live for another five to ten years. Eleven years later, on the occasion of his seventy-sixth year, Schoenberg received a letter from his boyhood friend Oskar Adler, who warned him that he should beware the number 76 (7 + 6). As Colin C. Sterne recounts, "The 13th day of July, the 7th month, fell on a Friday in 1951. Schoenberg, sickly and fearful, spent the entire day in bed. At fifteen minutes to midnight, his wife, Gertrud, entered his bedroom, to console him, perhaps, by pointing out how irrational his fears had been—the day was all but over, and it had passed without incident. Schoenberg raised his head, uttered the single word, 'Harmony,' and fell back dead. The time was 13 minutes to midnight."

. . .

IN 1977, I attended a performance by the New York Philharmonic at Avery Fisher Hall of *Final Alice,* a composition for soprano and orchestra by the contemporary American composer David Del Tredici, which is part of this composer's series of works based on Lewis Carroll's *Alice* books. Toward the end of this unabashedly romantic score, the soprano began slowly to count up in Italian—*"uno, due, tre"*—underlined by percussion sounds over a sustained A, then fading on the "tuning A" of the oboe with which the piece had begun. The singer (in this case the vocalist was Barbara Hendricks) continued to count up even more slowly—*"dieci, undici, dodici"*—and then, in a whisper, she spoke the word *"tredici . . ."* as the work came to a haunting close.

I had known many of Del Tredici's wonderfully innovative compositions, but until that moment I had never consciously realized that his last name was a number, and the number 13 at that. On my pilgrimage into the realm of 13 I obviously needed to speak to him. I wrote a letter to the composer, who suggested that I come to the Juilliard School, where he teaches music composition; and it was there that he talked to me about the number 13 and himself.

"Where does your name come from?" I asked.

"My sister Ann has been doing research on our family name and making connections with all of our old relatives," Del Tredici told me. "My father's mother left Italy when she was sixteen. Her husband died when he was thirty-two, and we lost touch with the other side of the family. But there are Del Tredicis who live in San Francisco, and Ann has been in contact with them.

"All the Del Tredicis seem to be related and to have come from an area in Italy called *Tredici Comuni* [The thirteen Municipalities], north of Verona. Ann found a reference to these municipalities in an Italian dictionary that states: 'Following the immigration of very poor woodsmen, sheep herders, and mountain-dwellers from the mountains of Bavaria onto the Lessini Plateau in the Venetian Republic (13th century), some autonomous municipalities reaching thirteen in number were created.' And Ann sent me a note in which she wrote that she was trying to reconcile the use of the singular article *(Del)* in front of a plural *(Tredici):*

> One would expect *dei Tredici* or *de' Tredici,* just like *dei Medici* or *de' Medici.* So it occurred to me that it may be an ellipsis for something like *Del* (commune dei) *Tredici* (Comuni) = *From the* (commune of the) *Thirteen* (Municipalities). Of course this is all purely speculative.

"So there you have it," the composer said to me.

"Were you aware that 13 was your name when you were young?" I asked.

"I don't know when I knew 13 was my name. It didn't make an impression. I didn't grow up in an ethnic area, so it didn't mean anything."

"Are you superstitious?"

"I never have been. In fact, I *like* the number 13. Since there are only twelve pitches, it is a magic *non*-note—after you've used up every real one. To me, 13 means *to go beyond.* It's one beyond midnight."

"Have you used 13 in works other than *Final Alice?*" I asked.

"In *An Alice Symphony,* which I wrote in 1969, I remember composing solo oboe entrances. Between each movement I'd put in an A, like a frame around a picture; and as I did more and more of them, I thought, 'I could have thirteen of these entrances!' So I counted them up and made it come out to thirteen. . . . I should also tell you that, for me, in this piece the oboe A is the musical equivalent of the 'dull reality' Lewis Carroll mentions in the text. When you hear that instrument playing A in both *An Alice Symphony* and *Final Alice,* it means that you're not yet, or are no longer, in Wonderland—you've woken up. When you hear the word *tredici,* it's all over.

"I've had thirteen elements in other pieces of mine, too—*Pop-Pourri* for solo soprano, chorus, rock group, and orchestra ends with thirteen tubular-bell strokes—but in *Final Alice* it was most out in the open, actually spoken, dramatized. This piece with its extravagant tonality says goodbye to my earlier style, which revolved more around atonality, additive rhythms, and numbers ('numbers' in the Schoenbergian sense of 'the twelve pitches, invert, repeat again . . .'). *Final Alice* isn't number-oriented at all because tonality can't be symmetrical. You have to write harmony 'by ear.' The number games I liked to play in my atonal works no longer fit. But *Final Alice* happened to conclude with a number that was my name, so I could, as it were, have my cake and eat it too.

"I did try and enhance the count, however. In the beginning of the count-up, the soprano speaks, then gradually she starts to whisper—you're not quite aware of where she's changing her voice—but only the word *tredici* is *really* whispered, so it gives it a ghostly quality. I enhance it further by having the orchestra members synchronously whisper the number. Thirteen becomes more magical than the numbers that preceded it.

"In Western music, there are only twelve half-steps, only twelve keys. There is no thirteenth note; thirteen is a new beginning—a free note. Thirteen is starting over again. Unlike Schoenberg, I actively *seek* 13 because after all it's my name. I'm truly stuck with the number!"

D URING MY CONVERSATION with David Del Tredici, he mentioned a poem he thought might interest me entitled *Powers of Thirteen,* written in 1984 by the contemporary poet John Hollander. The only major poem I could think of offhand that referred to the number 13 was Wallace Stevens's beautiful, Japanese-influenced "Thirteen Ways of Looking at a Blackbird." *Powers of Thirteen* is something quite different—a long work of 169 (13 × 13) stanzas consisting of 13 lines of 13 syllables each, resulting in a poem of 28,561 words (13^4). A meditation on diverse subjects and themes, the poem specifically examines the nature of the number 13:

Triskaidekaphobia across the centuries
Kept us seating one more at the table, even when
The extra one was silly or redundant or gross.
Moreover, the new arrangements—the sexes paired off,
The doubled sevens, the mysteries of ten and four—
Masqueraded as reasons, hiding always our fear
Of dangerous and pungent oddments behind the bright
And interesting arrangements that terror had us make.
Like grownups now, allowing the black cats to amble
Across our shadows in the forenoon without alarm,
We can at least, in a poor time for discourse, invite
Exactly whom we please, whom we need; it will be right
In a new shape, finished beyond the old completions.

John Hollander (his name, as he himself pointed out to me, consists of thirteen letters) is a Professor of English at Yale University and is the author of more than ten books of verse. He was the recipient of the Bollingen Prize in Poetry in 1983. When I spoke to the poet at his home in Connecticut, I asked him what his "powers of 13" referred to.

"There are several meanings for me," he said. "First, there are the algebraic powers. Then, whatever powers the number 13 might have to generate an entire poem about a great many things. And finally, the more distant sense of 'powers' referred to in the angelic orders—thrones, cherubim, seraphim, etc.—as if there are energetic powers of 13 that are presided over by that kind of power as well. But I was mainly thinking of the interplay between the exponential powers and the potential powers."

"What brought you to the number 13?" I asked.

"In a sense, I discovered it," Hollander replied. "I had written a poem

Number 13 Nightmares

The atomic bomb dropped on Hiroshima on August 6, 1945, was estimated to have been the equivalent of **13 kilotons of TNT.**

13 million gallons of chemical agents were dumped in Vietnamese soil during the Vietnam War.

On July 16, 1995, President Jacques-René Chirac of France publicly recognized his country's responsibility for rounding up some **13,000 Jewish men, women, and children** into the Vel d'Hir, an indoor cycling stadium. After being interned in the Paris suburb of Droncy, they were deported to death camps.

In Saudi Arabia, **13 judges** officiate in cases leading to the public beheadings of defendants found guilty of capital crimes.

Between June 1962 and January 1964, Albert H. DeSalvo, known as the Boston Strangler, killed **13 women** in Boston, Massachusetts. Tried and convicted in 1967, he was murdered in his jail cell.

some years before called 'Looking Ahead' that happened to be in thirteen-syllable lines. For a good many years after that I wrote purely syllabic verse—my book *Reflections on Espionage* was all in eleven-syllable lines—so that I had some of the effects of free verse but nevertheless a strict regimen. Then I wrote a poem called 'Speaking Plainly,' which not only was in thirteen-syllable lines but also had thirteen lines to each stanza. I was fascinated by what had gone on in it and what I'd learned from doing it, and I realized I had found a kind of space or form that was good for me to work in. And that poem became a sequence in *Powers of Thirteen*. At any rate, I had found this form, and I thought it would be fun to try to do something in it. And of course the first thing that came to me was that I was working with a sonnet manqué—my stanza lacked a line—but I decided to see what would happen if one tried sonnet-like things in this form. And so I fell into writing these 169 stanzas, which took me over a year and a half."

"Have you ever been superstitious about the number 13?" I asked.

"No, never," said Hollander. "I was brought up on the West Side of Manhattan in one of those prewar apartment buildings in which very often there was no floor 13. When I was six years old I remember asking my father, 'On the elevator, why is there 12 and 14 but not 13?' And he told me, 'A lot of people are superstitious about the number 13 and they don't want to live on the thirteenth floor.' 'But if they live on the fourteenth floor they're living on the thirteenth.' And he said, 'Exactly.' So I realized that people who were superstitious about 13 would be delighted to live on the thirteenth floor if it was *called* 14 . . . or sometimes 12A, my mother told me, in some buildings. And since there was nothing wrong with living on the thirteenth floor but only something wrong with living on what was *called* the thirteenth floor, I had, even at the age of six, sorted the situation out myself."

"In your poem," I said, "you mention the clock striking 13."

"That's an old school or summer camp joke," Hollander said. " 'What time is it when the clock strikes 13? Time to have the clock fixed.' "

"You also talk about a character named Crazy Hans who sits on the sidewalk strumming his crazy guitar that is tuned to a thirteen-tone scale in which 'the octaves alone are true.' "

"I was thinking," Hollander explained, "of a thirteen-tone scale such that you can have perfectly in-tune octaves and then divide up everything into thirteen so that absolutely nothing would sound like a whole tone. Put it this way: 13 throws the 12 system out of joint; and all of this is in a sense a way of giving 13 a certain kind of imaginative power—going beyond the scale but not altering its overall shape. I would have to say that ultimately, in my poem, 13 is a trope for originality. I think that 13 is the poem's lucky number. For me there was the technical matter of how a purely thirteen-syllable line could liberate me and bring forth certain ideas, themes, and feelings. In this sense, 13 was a kind of charm or spell calling up the whole poem and everything in it.

"I wanted to explore thirteenness. And I suppose that's why there is another figure in it—someone called 'you' who's a combination muse and reader. It's a female figure, a kind of general reader accompanying the speaker on walks and who is always being addressed."

"Sometimes," I mentioned, "I took this 'you' to be the number 13 itself, as in the lines: 'You use me for my purposes I'm ignorant of. / You are given to utter what I must intimate . . . /I improvise over your recurring undersong.' "

"I think so," said Hollander. "Well, I never thought so before. It's one of those insights you really can't have about your own work. I would never have thought to put it that way. Given what you're interested in with regard to the subject of your own book, I could say, Yes, he would say that. But as a matter of fact what you say is right.

"I could imagine having a dream in which I encounter that 'you' I invented in the poem having an occasional dialogue with me, and my saying to her in the dream, 'What's your name?' and she saying to me, 'Thirteen.' What I had imagined that creature to be was imagination itself, the metaphoric, the figurative—that which was therefore the most free."

WHEN I FIRST BEGAN THINKING about the number 13, I paused to consider the following: At the time of writing this book, my age was a multiple of 13; the number of my apartment building was made up of the numbers 4 + 2 + 7; my telephone number included the number 13 and a multiple of 13 in it; and the numerological value of my last name was also equal to the number 13. So I decided to make an appointment with John Francavilla, a numerologist who lives in New York City.

Numerologists believe that the universe is governed by numerical laws, that each number has special powers and qualities, and that one can use numbers to define and analyze the strengths and weaknesses of human character, as well as to predict the future. The numbers of a person's name and birthday are considered to be of primary importance and are determined by the matching of each letter in a name with a number (C = 3, O = 6, T = 2); and those numbers with two or more digits are reduced by

Two Suicides and the Number 13

From the *Yorkshire Post*, May, 1960: "A note left by a window cleaner who was found dead in a gas-filled room at his home said: 'It just needed to rain today **Friday the 13th** for me to make up my mind.' "

On the evening of **Friday the 13th** in January 1995, the iconoclastic artist Ray Johnson jumped from a highway bridge over Sag Harbor Cove in Long Island, New York, and was last seen by two teenage boys backstroking in the freezing waters. Several hours before his death, Johnson checked into a nearby motel and specifically asked for **room 247**, whose digits add up to **13**, as do the digits of the time he was spotted in the water by the two boys, **7:15 P.M.**, and as do the digits in his age, **67**. (The day before his death, Ray Johnson had phoned a friend and told him, "I have a new project, the biggest I've ever undertaken, the most important one in my life.")

adding their digits (M = 13 = 1 + 3 = 4). The title of Florence Evylinn Campbell's classic work on this subject perfectly conveys the numerologist's credo: *Your Days Are Numbered*.

John Francavilla is a man of great personal warmth and a decided mystical bent. "Your quest regarding the number 13," he told me straightaway on my entering his apartment, "is important on both a personal and a wider level because of the need to get rid of superstitions and to start understanding our role as human life-forces. . . . Do you know much about numerology?" he asked me. "Very little," I replied. John invited me to sit down at a small table, and he sat opposite me. There was a feeling of the early Middle Ages in the room. Behind John stood a manikin in black medieval armor, and there were paintings of dragons on the wall and dragon prints on the rug. On the other side of the room sat a pumpkin on a table in preparation for Halloween.

"In numerology, the name and birthdate are the two coordinates of the psyche," John explained to me. "The name is the logos, the place; the birthdate is the time. What we are is the time and the place coming together. When we make a hologram, we take one laser beam and split it into two, and those two interface with the object, causing its appearance on film. Similarly, we are two forces—time and space—that crisscross. The name is the space we inhabit, the birthdate is the time that that instant occurs. Numbers and letters are the same, and always have been: A = 1, B = 2, and so on. We can add your name up—the vowels separately, the consonants separately, the whole thing together. Different totals give different information.

"Now, the correspondence between the name and the birthdate concerns the number 3, which is of course in the number 13. The birthdate has three parts to it—the month, day, and year; so does the name—first, middle, and last. The full name is called the destiny number, the vowels create the soul number, the consonants create the personality number. So we have

A Peaceful 13

On **September 13,** 1993, Yasir Arafat and Yitzhak Rabin shook hands on the White House lawn in Washington, D.C., after signing a declaration of principles for a historic agreement on interim Palestinian self-rule.

these trinities occurring in our names and birthdays. The number 3 is the divine triangle. Before physical incarnation, the ideal exists; the number 3 pertains to this.

"The number 13 deals with the issues of self, trinity, and transcendence. And why we're so hung up with it in our civilization is because people are afraid of change. They're afraid of the notion of time. Thirteen relates to the aspect of time: Think of the symbol of the Grim Reaper in the thirteenth card of the Tarot deck. We feel that time is going to run out and we're going to die. So death and the number 13 become synonymous. Judas was the thirteenth apostle. He brought on the death of Christ by betraying him. The number 3 in numerology corresponds to the planet Jupiter—expansion, good luck, speech, dance, poetry, music, delight, travel, merriment. But there's a limit to it, we're told, because if we add the 1 and 3 together we get the 4. And that means there's only so much time we're going to have. That's how our human consciousness perceives it.

"When people are born on the 13th or have 13 as an aspect of their numbers, they will feel closed or boxed in. In their previous incarnations, which they're unconscious of, they did not express themselves as fully as they might have: 'I could have done this, I could have done that.' They didn't make use of their time. Laziness. The negative side of the 3 with the 1 in front of it represents the ego sitting back saying, 'I could do all these things and I'm just going to goof off.' They let time slip away. So death/time/the demon are all associated. Why should the number 13 be so unlucky to so many people? Because of its association with death and, most important, with the idea of time and with using time correctly. Any fear and superstition attached to this number is our human situation that we have to overcome. In our lives we all go to the fourteenth floor and deny the thirteenth, but each of us has to confront the number 13."

John proceeded to do my numerological chart with its soul, karmic, maturity, and pinnacle numbers, which he interpreted and elaborated on for me. I withhold his remarks, not so much because they are personal, but because there are fewer things more benumbing than listening to the nuances of a stranger's numerological or astrological chart.

"You're coming to terms with the number 13," John said to me in more general terms, "because your last name adds up to that. Your *full* name, however, is a 4, which results from adding 2 + 2, not 1 + 3. And 22 is the master number that goes along with the power to synthesize ideas of a spiritual nature and put them into a form that will allow you to convey them effectively. But you have to confront the number 13 at this stage in your life. Why? You've written twelve books and you're on to your thirteenth. But it's also because you're now dealing with the deeper notions of what this represents. It's the beginning of a whole other way of writing, a whole other journey, a whole other twelve books! It's a symbolic death and resurrection, dealing with your mortality and with one of man's deepest superstitions regarding this particular cipher. You start off as an investigator, and because you're investigating this phenomenon it reflects back elements within you."

"So I investigate, but I become investigated," I commented.

"Exactly. You interview me and I interview you. The number 13 needs to be confronted in all of us. We have to ask ourselves: Why do we feel hesitant about this vibration? What is it doing? Then look at our own lives and see where we stand."

· · ·

La Morte (Marseilles Tarot deck).

THE TAROT CARDS, consisting of twenty-two allegorical images called the major arcana or enigmas—The Magician, the High Priestess, the Hermit, the Hanged Man, etc.—and fifty-six minor arcana, date at least from the fourteenth century; they are said not only to reflect an esoteric knowledge derived from Hermetism and Kabbalistic mysticism but also to map a path of initiation by revealing man's inner evolution from ignorance to enlightenment.

The number 13 card in the Tarot deck is the Death card, most often depicted as a skeleton with a scythe, harvesting a crop of dismembered heads, hands, and feet—the typical Grim Reaper with its skull mask and skeleton suit of the medieval mystery play, in whose presence all of humanity, king or commoner, is equal. According to John Francavilla, the number 13 card in the Tarot deck has the same significance as the number 13 itself. "In the Pythagorean sense," he told me, "numbers were living beings and they were later translated into the Tarot cards to give them shape and form. The cards are the way people interpret them."

In *Tarot of the Spirit,* Pamela Eakins provides a book to accompany the Tarot cards painted by her mother, the artist Joyce Eakins. It is one of a proliferation of contemporary Tarot decks reinterpreting the traditional images. In one recent deck called the PoMo Tarot, subtitled "A Postmodern Deck for Navigating the Next Millennium," its iconographer and creator, Brian Williams, presents a number 13 card in which Death is a skull with a pair of wraparound sunglasses over its eye sockets and a lit cigarette lodged between its teeth. No matter how up-to-date the Tarot cards may be, their traditional meanings are never lost sight of.

Visiting Pamela Eakins in her home near Half Moon Bay, California, I asked her about the Tarot's unnerving Death card. "The easiest way to put it," she told me, "is that from a spiritual perspective, death precedes a spiritual rebirth, which is called the second birth. So this 'death' is what happens to the individual before that takes place. You can think of it as the death of our everyday personality. It's common to shamanic systems the world over. What the shaman must face is his or her own death before the enlightenment state can enter, and then the person can move out of the space of death, reborn as a holy one, a healer, an enlightened be-

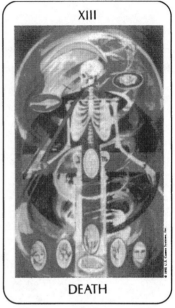

XIII

DEATH

Number 13 card in the Tarot of the Spirit deck, painted by Joyce Eakins.

ing. And that's really what death in the Tarot is about—the death of small things, incidents, projects, and then the rebirth that grows out of that. You let something go, and something new comes in."

"What about literal, 'physical' death?" I asked.

"The card does represent physical death," Eakins said, "but if I were doing a reading, I'd be very hesitant to call it that. It depends on what's happening in a reading. Just last night I was at a book signing for *Tarot of the Spirit* and I passed out some Tarot cards from our deck. I let the people there draw out some cards, and only one person didn't show me what card he got. Today, I was going through the deck and realized that the only card missing was the Death card. I had told the audience at the book signing that every card in the Tarot was good, and if one got a card like the Death card one shouldn't leave until speaking to me so that I could explain what it meant. Obviously the person who got that card was too afraid to do that. Physical death is the question at the heart of all religions and spiritual traditions, it's at the heart of our being, really. That's the question we all face from the time we're about thirteen years old. It starts sinking in then."

"There's that number 13 again," I commented.

"Yes," Eakins said, "I think that 13, the age of puberty, is a very big transition, a time when we start to realize our mortality."

Classical 13's

Agamemnon was murdered by his wife, Clytemnestra, on the **13th of Gamelion** (January).

Odysseus, **the 13th of his group** of companions, is the only one to have escaped the devouring appetite of the Cyclops Polyphemus.

The Amazon Queen Minythyla tried to mate with Alexander the Great during a period of **13 days.**

Oenomaus, the father of Hippodamia, killed **13 of her suitors** before Pelops won her.

Philip II of Macedonia was assassinated shortly after he allowed a statue of himself to be erected along with those of the 12 gods of Olympus, making **13 statues** in all.

"Don't you think there may well be a connection between puberty and death?" I wondered.

"It could well be," she replied. "The awakening of sexuality is connected with the continuation of the species, and where we were once at the baby end, we're now looking forward to the other end. It comes through the music and poetry kids pay attention to. They're confronted with it and they say, 'What's the point of living when you're just going to die anyway?' And they have to discover the small things in life that are going to make their lives worthwhile. So I don't think it's an accident that the Death card is number 13.

"Physical death is at the heart of the mysteries. It's interesting that in the Tarot, death doesn't appear at the end of the deck, it's in the middle; and that says that if you come to terms with your death it will give you a lease on life in a new way. Coming to terms with what it means to die means you're coming to terms with what it means to live. And if you follow the path of the Tarot, you can learn to activate your awareness of your own death, which gives you, in a certain sense, a chance to come to terms with death and to know whether you think there's something beyond that. In working deeply with Tarot, you learn how to go into death intentionally, the way shamans do, to experience that place of complete stillness in meditation, which some people feel is a kind of death. Through meditation, we enter into the place of dreams and journeys, then we move beyond that. We move into a deathlike state where we begin to come to grips with physical death and with what that means. This is a very individual process.

"For people who are unknowledgeable about the spiritual path and the deep meaning of things, the number 13 may seem to be unlucky; for people who are knowledgeable and conscious, it would seem to be very lucky. In the former case, when you go through a change of great magnitude—a near-death experience, say—it disrupts the status quo of your life and social relations. However, if you go into that *consciously,* it can be the most magnificent kind of transformation. That is what the 13 experience is all about. You discard your shell and then you're so tender and everything is fragile. This is the mid-life crisis for many people. If you think of the twenty-two major arcana, the higher cards in the Tarot deck, as a single life span, then this number 13 is somewhere in or just after the middle. You wake up and say, Something's wrong, and *then* you begin. . . . So the 13 has three meanings: at thirteen years old, at mid-life, and at the end of life. It appears at all these times."

"What do the images in the various Death cards—traditional and modern—represent?" I asked.

"In our *Tarot of the Spirit* deck," Eakins said, "the fish, which is the sign of the Hebrew letter *nun* that is associated with this card, represents regener-

Patriotic 13's

That 13 brings ill-luck is mere tradition,

Yea, even more, 'tis foolish superstition—

For 13, lucky number runs,

Through all our Country's ripening suns—

'Tis for Our Land an omen good—

For Peace—Liberty—Brotherhood!

—from **Lucky 13,** a mini-epic written by Maurice Walter in 1919

The **13 American colonies** banded together to revolt against England and formed the United States of America. The Declaration of Independence was signed by **13 representatives,** and a flag with **13 stars** was made on **January 13,** 1794.

France announced support for the 13 colonies on **June 13,** 1778.

ation and immortal life. The rose on a platter represents purity and inno-
cence, the consciousness of the fool. Because being born requires a certain
childlike characteristic, a beginner's mind. Think of Ingmar Bergman's *The
Seventh Seal* in which at the end of the film the characters are lined up and
dancing with Death, and the last one in the row is the Fool—the Fool is
dancing with Death.

"In our Tarot deck, the cross of equal arms represents the intersection
of spirit, heart, mind, and body, and right in the center of that is a devel-
oping foetus. This foetus suggests the importance of achieving a balance between your spiritual path, your heart, your relationships, your feelings,
your intellectual endeavors, and your body. And if you're not balanced,
you're going to be pulled into a sort of death.

Thomas Jefferson was born on **April 13,** 1743.

In the Great Seal of the United States, **the number 13** is used **13
times** — in the number of stars over the eagle's head; the number of
clouds around the stars; the number of arrows, stripes, leaves, and
berries in the olive branches; the number of feathers in the eagle's tail;
the number of steps of the pyramid; the number of letters in *E Pluribus
Unum* and *Annuit Coeptus;* and the number of letters (13 × 3) in the title:
"The Coat of Arms of the United States of America."

In February 1995, **130 years** (13 × 10) after the conclusion of the Civil
War, the Senate and House of the State of Mississippi "officially"
endorsed **the 13th Amendment** to the U.S. Constitution, which
declares, "Neither slavery nor involuntary servitude . . . shall exist
within the United States." Mississippi was the last of nine Civil War
holdout-states to approve the amendment.

"More traditionally, the two dismembered figures—a male and a female—represent the death and dismemberment of humanity, which you can look at on the spiritual/psychological level or as actual death and rebirth. We should remember that a central aspect of the shamanic experience the world over is dismemberment, symbolic or actual. Sometimes, for example, in the shamanic experience of death and rebirth, the shaman's soul travels into the underworld. There it is cared for by the bird-of-prey mother, his overseer, who cuts the soul into very small pieces that are fed to evil spirits of disease and death. Then, when the bird-of-prey mother sees that the shaman has had enough, she reassembles the shaman; and when he emerges from the experience he is reborn a holy one. And because his soul—and his body symbolically—has been fed to the demons of disease and death, he understands disease and death and becomes a healer. The lesson is: You have to be dismembered to remember who you are. The adept remembers that he or she is an immortal being and has access through subconscious channels to all that has ever been, all that is and ever shall be."

"What about the scythe?" I asked.

"The scythe that Death is carrying," replied Eakins, "is a blade and it represents the mind, in the sense of 'being sharp as a blade,' 'getting to the point.' The Grim Reaper is a state of mind. Let's call it a skeleton wielding consciousness. We can see the scythe as cutting out, taking away that which is extraneous, forms and structures that bind you to the past or the present. Rending the veil from the path of your soul."

"Isn't the scythe also a crescent moon?" I wondered.

"That scythe is definitely a moon," she said. "The moon reflects the sun, and the sun is the source of all light. So, too, death is only a reflection of something that is much deeper. Death equals the blade, the mind. So the whole idea of death and birth has to do with constraints of the human mind. But there's constraint beyond which the human mind cannot even begin to understand, which is the life force itself. And that's what death itself represents—the spark of life that continues to exist through all the births and deaths.

"Traditionally, too, the moon represents going down into the darkness of the subconscious. And that is what the Death card represents. The lunar image has to do with a journey into the deep subconscious to confront yourself and understand your cycles, your connections to the universe."

"Since we're all skeletons," I said, "isn't the Death figure somehow a mirror of ourselves?"

"What else are we?" she replied. "What is in the empty space? Our task as human beings is to find out if there's anything in the space. To get into this space requires that you transcend the teachings of your culture and everything you believe to be true. You venture out on your own, and it's a journey that you can only do by yourself to discover what's real."

THE *I CHING*, or the Chinese *Book of Changes*, is a three-thousand-year-old divination text and a repository of astonishing wisdom. The book consists of sixty-four different six-lined images called hexagrams that are said to "describe the conditions and attitudes we encounter throughout our lives." The Chinese gave each hexagram a name and description and added stories and proverbs to illustrate their meaning. By addressing a question to the *I Ching* and tossing six coins, one discovers the appropriate hexagram whose meaning is inherent in that moment of time.

I was curious to know what the *I Ching* had to say about the number 13. So I turned to a new version of the work entitled *The I Ching Made Easy: Be Your Own Psychic Advisor Using the World's Oldest Oracle* by Roderic Sorrell and Amy Max Sorrell. I turned the book to Hexagram 13, which reads: "COMPAN-IONSHIP/SHARING/COOPERATION: *All for one and one for all . . . Out in the open with friends.*" But was there any inextricable connection between the meaning of this hexagram and the number 13, in the way that the Death card

Taxing 13's

The first constitutional federal income tax law was passed by Congress in **1913** upon the ratification of the 16th Amendment to the Constitution ("The Congress shall have power to lay and collect taxes on incomes, from whatever source derived . . .").

Jerry Brown, running in the 1994 Democratic primaries for President of the United States, proposed a **13 percent flat tax** and a **13 percent value-added tax.** (If only he had suggested 17!)

and 13 are inseparable in the Tarot? So I put this question to Roderic Sorrell, the coauthor of *The I Ching Made Easy,* who lives in Bisbee, Arizona.

"Let me first explain," said Sorrell, "that the hexagram is a binary number with six digits in it, ranging from 000000 to 111111. The hexagram is a binary number because it's made up of 0 and 1—your two binary digits—or yin and yang, such that yin equals 0 and yang equals 1. There are sixty-four combinations of yin and yang, but the traditional arrangement of the hexagrams does not follow this binary order. Hexagram 1, for example, consists of six yang lines; in the binary counting, however, that's Hexagram 64. The traditional Hexagram 13, to give another example, corresponds to binary number 61. Therefore the traditional order doesn't follow the binary sequence. So I simply set the hexagrams together following the binary system, taking the yin as 0 and yang as 1; and instead of placing them vertically (the Chinese wrote vertically), I placed them horizontally. And thus the number 13 comes out to be Hexagram 55.

"Now, Hexagram 55 reads: 'PLEN-TY/HARVEST/ABUNDANCE: *Make hay while the sun shines . . . Be like the noonday* sun.' The Chinese character *Feng*, which is used to describe this hexagram, shows a basket of grain over a wine cup. It means: ripe, abundant to the point of overflowing, fullness, or culmination. On the surface, this doesn't seem to have a great deal to do with death, as does the Tarot card number 13. But of course, in the Tarot, Death holds a scythe—a symbol of harvest—and harvest is something that comes when things have reached their peak. Death is the culmination of the activity of a lifetime. At the moment of our death, our life flashes before our eyes, everything we have done is gathered together, the harvest of a lifetime. Every activity reaches a point of fullness and completion when it must pass on to the next stage, in which it becomes overripe and begins to decay. Even a letter to a friend can become overworked and lose its freshness. Exercise taken past its peak leads to exhaustion. So there's a sense of connection with the Tarot there.

"When you do a reading in our book, by the way, you ask a question, then throw six coins and get a hexagram and one moving line. The line is the primary piece of advice; that is what you pay attention to. It occurs within the general sense of the hexagram as a whole, but if you want to get it down to the basic phrase, that phrase is one line."

"Could you give me an example of how you would interpret Line 1 of Hexagram 55, which in your book reads: 'Meeting your partner, good for ten days'?" I asked.

" 'Good for ten days,' " Sorrell told me, "means that everything has its expiration date. A time to live and a time to die. Doing the right thing, but at the wrong time, will just not work. Now, if your *I Ching* reading is about taking a trip with someone and you get this line of the hexagram, then it means that the trip will be good for a certain period of time. And yes, that he or she may want something from you as indicated in some of the translations for this particular line. . . . Incidentally, I've studied about thirty or forty translations of the *I Ching*, and I have a data base of close to four thousand readings in order to try to say, OK, if this works, what is the consensus on this, which translation represents most accurately what really is happening? And I find I can best judge that by taking a reading that seems to reflect the condition with an actual life situation."

"Line 2 of Hexagram 55 reads: 'The curtains are so thick that even at noon the lamps must be lit.' "

"We hide behind our curtains and screens," Sorrell stated. "To a point, our facade or public face protects us. If it is taken to excess, we become hidden, introverted, and stagnant. We cannot cut ourselves off from life in a vain attempt to prevent its influence on us—an influence that includes change and impermanence.

"I remember reading that line out to a friend, and she said, 'Ah, that's what Richard Nixon did, he lived in California, but he had the air conditioner on to make the place cold enough so that he could have a fire.' That's like being so rich that you can have these very thick curtains and then have to light the lamps at noon in order to see your way around, whereas normally anyone would open the curtains. It's an extravagant gesture, it's an abundance of excess."

"Line 3 reads: 'So many flags darken the sky; a broken right arm.' "

"The flags darkening the sky," said Sorrell, "represent the froth and noise that obscure our view of the light. Too much information obscures wisdom. You have gone beyond the point of completion.

"My grandfather read just one book, *Scott's Last Expedition;* he read it and read it and said, 'Everything I need is in that book; it tells of heroism, of how to get on with other people.' I myself would need another two lifetimes just to read the books I have in my library. We no longer read, we skim. And so we are getting a little out of a lot instead of a lot out of a little. We're debasing ourselves terribly. I think our society is rapidly moving toward a tremendous state of overwhelm. Which is the condition of Line 3."

"Line 4 reads: 'Heavy curtains cut out all the light.' "

"Do you remember the 1994 elections when the Republicans took over

Congress?" said Sorrell. "That's the hexagram line they got! It means that you're
going to win because there's abundance—
an abundance of votes—but that's not necessarily going to clarify the situation. You
get that line, but from then on you're on
your own, you have to figure it out yourself. 'Heavy curtains . . .' What does that
mean? Again, you're back to the image of
very rich, lush velvet curtains. But they cut
out the light. Again, it's an overwhelm;
someone is so rich in information, in prej-
udices, in furniture, that he can be iso-
lated, he can't see the simplest thing in
front of him, which is the sunlight shining
through the window."

"Line 5 reads: 'Your shining inner light
wins blessings.' "

"The sun is now in your heart," Sorrell
stated. "Inside and outside are one. You do
not resist the flow of life that includes
change and impermanence. In most cases,
Line 5 is the most favorable line of a hexagram. In Line 1, you're at the beginning of
a situation; in Line 2, you're in a better position but you're still on a low point; and in
the next two lines you gradually work up-
ward. So Line 5 is generally the most
promising: it's central, it's not on the edge,
not jammed up in the middle, it's nicely

Apollo 13

The ill-fated **Apollo 13**
mission was launched on
April 11, 1970, at **1313
hours** Central Time from
Pad 39 (13 × 3), and had
to be aborted on **April
13** after the explosion of
an oxygen tank serving
the command ship. Three
of the sleeping periods
scheduled for the
astronauts were supposed
to start at **13 minutes**
past the hour, as was one
of the possible
splashdown times.

The film **Apollo 13**
grossed **$26 million**
(13 × 2) in its first
weekend showings in the
United States.

placed. Here, your inner wisdom shines from within, you have something to celebrate, you have the support of able helpers."

"Finally, Line 6 reads: 'Peering in at the palace gate, empty for three years.' "

"The palace is empty," said Sorrell. "The spirit has left the body. Maybe you are hanging around as a ghost, but really it is time to move on. Here, you have gracefully retired from the scene, you're no longer the head of a company, your son has taken over. Or else you refuse to let go of the controls and are doddering around and making a fool of yourself and being a stupid old tyrant. Here, the palace is empty, perhaps you're still hiding away inside, but the power has gone somewhere else—it's gone to the younger generation or to a more powerful source. There's a sense of abandoned grandeur."

"So what then do you see as the overall meaning of Hexagram 55?" I asked.

"The hexagram suggests that abundance can be a ripe fruit, but a few days later it's overripe. If abundance isn't shared, it can obscure your clarity of mind. Are the curtains going to cut out the light?"

"Could this hexagram be taken as a warning or a call to awareness?" I wondered.

"A call to awareness," replied Sorrell. "It's not that adversity is 'bad' or prosperity 'good.' The former isn't bad if it gives you an opportunity to discover more about what you're capable of doing in difficult circumstances. And there can be good fortune in adversity. So no situation has the clarity of 'good' or 'bad' to it. We should see the situation as it is, and then respond to it sanely. A hexagram doesn't have a simple meaning. Hexagram 55 says: Make hay while the sun shines, but if you make too much of it, you will lose it, it will slip through your hands. It's an abundance to be enjoyed right now, it's an opportunity not to be missed.

"So how does Hexagram 55 in the *I Ching* relate to the number 13 and the vision of death? Hexagram 55 speaks about *life*. This hexagram is about living life to the fullest. Death is inevitable. Life can be a harvest or famine. We may not get this chance again, so we must be decisive and make it happen. This advises us to use the opportunity of our precious human life and to grab the brass ring.

"And if you meditate on each one of the sixty-four hexagrams, as we've been doing with Hexagram 55, you'll fill a very worthy sixty-four days of your life."

IN FEBRUARY 1995, Jacqueline Mitton of the Royal Astronomical Society in England announced the existence of a thirteenth astrological sign called Ophiuchus, which is supposed to fit somewhere between Scorpio and Sagittarius. Newspapers around the world ran the story, pondering what the implications would be for astrological horoscopes, compatible sun signs, birthstones, etc. I wanted to get some clarification about this "thirteenth" astrological sign, so I got in touch with Robert Hand in Orleans, Massachusetts. Hand is one of the founders of Astrolabe (a company that creates software for doing astrological calculations) and is currently working on translations of classical and medieval texts on astrology. He straightaway informed me that this "thirteenth sign" was actually a nonissue.

"The twelve signs of the zodiac," Hand explained, "have their origin in a schematic allocation of the paths of the sun to twelve constellations. Why twelve? Because there are roughly twelve lunations in a year—there are thirteen lunar revolutions but twelve lunations. [A lunar revolution is the time the moon takes to complete one orbit of the earth relative to a fixed point such as the distant stars; but a lunation is the time between two new moons.]

"When this convention of dividing the path of the sun, also known as the ecliptic, into twelve equal divisions took place, there was no apparent evidence that anybody knew about the procession of the equinoxes, so that

Royal 13's

When Princess Margaret was born in Scotland's Glamis Castle on August 21, 1930, palace officials delayed the registration of her birth for three days until another baby was born, so that the princess's registration number wouldn't be **13.**

When Queen Elizabeth II paid a visit to West Germany in 1965, the number of the platform at Duisburg railway station, from which she was about to depart, was changed **from 13 to 12A.**

When the Spanish princess Elena de Borbon celebrated her marriage on March 18, 1995, to the banker Jaime de Marichalar y Saenz de Tejada, he participated in an old Castilian custom by ritually pouring **13 gold coins** into the hands of his bride as a sign that their goods would be held in common *(bienes con juntos)*.

In 1886, Maria Christina, Queen Regent of Spain, was persuaded by the antisuperstition Thirteen Club of New York City to ignore the pleas of her ministers and christen her son **"Alfonso XIII."** (The unpopular Alfonso later had to abdicate the throne.)

The French monarch **Louis XIII,** who declared the **number 13** to be his favorite number, married Anna of Austria when she was **13 years old.**

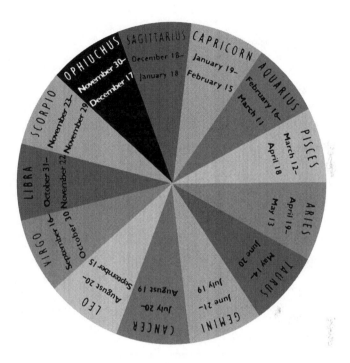

Ophiuchus—the thirteenth astrological sign?

very early on, around 200 B.C., there was no real distinction between dividing the zodiac according to the vernal point or according to the constellations, because they were roughly coincident. So what happened was that a few people began saying, 'Hey, look, this is eventually going to be a problem.' And two decisions were made. One was made in India, where they decided to take the *constellations* as their fixed point; the other was made in the West where, following Ptolemy, people decided to take the seasons as the fixed point. So our zodiac is a seasonal one. Unfortunately, the names

of constellations that once occupied the twelve divisions of the year got assigned to those seasonal divisions; but now they no longer coincide. So we
have the spectacle of an astrologer referring to a point of the sky as being
in the *sign* of Aries when it is in the *constellation* of Pisces. What we've really got is two different zones of the sky called Aries.

"Astrologers have been aware of this from the beginning. This is not
news, even though astronomers like to pretend that we're ignorant of it, and
that we're really using the wrong zodiac. What we're really doing is using a
different zodiac, not the wrong one, a zodiac which has nothing whatsoever
to do with the fixed stars. It's based on seasonal, not sidereal, rhythms."

"So what does this all add up to?" I asked.

"Not a damn thing," said Hand. "The problem here is that astronomers
like to trot out the business of the zodiac recession and the constellations
every so often because they think it's acutely embarrassing to astrologers.
And our reaction invariably is, 'Oh God, not again!' Because, frankly, we're
very much aware of it. The astrological community even has an ongoing de-
bate about the two twelve-fold zodiacal frameworks—one based on the
stars, one based on the seasons. I think there is an increasing consensus that
they are simply different kinds of zodiacs to be used for different purposes."

"Could you say something about the relationship between the moon and
the number 13?" I asked.

"I think the fundamental reason for the number 13 being a lunar number," Hand stated, "is because the sun moves approximately one degree a
day while the moon moves thirteen degrees. Do you have any idea how
close the average daily motion of the moon is to 13? It's very close—13.1
degrees, 13.2 if rounded correctly. The sun and moon are in an almost perfect thirteen-to-one ratio. It's a clear pattern that the ancients themselves
noticed. I have found about five different techniques from ancient astrology
that are solidly based on that ratio. All of this has made 13 a moon number
and 12 a sun number.

"More important, there's a whole methodology for reading charts of night-born people that is quite different from reading charts of day-born people. A night chart is affected by the moon, and the moon is much more powerful in the night chart than in the day chart, and the sun is correspondingly weaker in the night chart. That body of work became completely screwed-up in the Middle Ages, and you only find fragments of it in recent astrology. But in the ancient Greek era there was a completely worked-out methodology for reading the two charts differently. When we apply this now in our practical work, we find that it makes quite a difference. It appears that a lot of astrological effects are wiped out by ignoring the distinction between day and night births. If you're going to emphasize sun signs, which I don't think is a totally hot idea, then for night births you should emphasize moon signs."

"Are you surprised that in our culture the number 13 is considered unlucky?" I asked.

"Not particularly," he said. "I've pretty well decided that it was a bad rap given 13 because of the moon; I don't think it's all that farfetched to attribute the unlucky nature of 13 to the repression of the moon goddess. Moon states in general are emotional or psychic or nonlinear. Thirteen is associated with the moon in our minds, and that's what gives it that aura of weirdness. It's a product of the active repression of the feminine that we see quite clearly occurring in the Middle Ages.

"Now, there's nothing antifeminine in anything that's solar. Antifeminine goes with what's anti-lunar. Merely stating the masculine is not antifeminine. If you *repress* the feminine it's antifeminine. If you've been down for a couple of thousand years, like the lunar number 13, and you find out that you're at least equal to the solar number 12, there will obviously be a backlash against the latter and what it symbolizes. But the last thing we need is to have either a matriarchy or a patriarchy anymore. We don't want to keep the pendulum swinging; the goal is to stop the pendulum."

"BLAME IT ON THE MOON." "Blame it on the moon goddess."
"Blame it on the number 13." In song, folklore, mythology, and archaeol-
ogy, the connections between the moon, the physiological life of a woman,
and the number 13 are pervasive and universal. There are thirteen moons
in a lunar year; and the time the moon takes to complete one cycle of its
phases (new moon/waxing moon/full moon/waning moon) is 29.5306
days, and is called a synodic or lunar month. The mean length of the female
menstrual cycle is between 28 and 29 days, and it is therefore not surprising that the word for month and the word for menstruation are the same
or closely related in many languages. In English, the word "menstruation"
derives from the Greek *mēnē* (moon) and the Latin *mensis* (month). In
French, a term for the menstrual period is *le moment de la lune,* and in Germany, peasants used to refer to it simply as *der Mond.* In his book *The Mothers,* Robert Briffault states that the Congolese peoples use the word *njonde*
and the Mandingo peoples the word *carro* for both moon and menstruation.
The Maori speak of menses as *mata marama* (moon sickness). In Babylonian
mythology, the moon goddess Ishtar was thought to be menstruating during the full moon.

The waxing and waning of the moon was an early means of measure-
ment of time longer than a day, which could be measured by the sun. According to the pioneering work of the archaeologist Alexander Marshak,
people during the Upper Paleolithic used a system of lunar notation by
making notches or markings on stone, bones, and antlers. The famous Goddess of Laussel—a seventeen-inch Stone Age Venus (c. 22,000–18,000
B.C.) carved on a block of limestone—holds in her right hand a bison's
horn, crescent-shaped like the moon, on which thirteen notches indicate
both the thirteen days of the waxing moon and the thirteen months of the
lunar year; while with her left hand she points to her swelling womb. In the

The Goddess of Laussel (c. 22,000–18,000 B.C.), Dordogne, France.

Design by Peter Nilson.

words of Joseph Campbell, "It may be that the initial observation that gave birth in the mind of man to a mythology of one mystery informing earthly and celestial things was the recognition of an accord between these two 'time-factored' orders: the celestial order of the waxing moon and the earthly order of the womb." Not for nothing can the shape of the number 3 in the number 13 be seen as two parturient crescent moons!

The moon was the measure (from the Latin word *mensura*) of cycles of time, particularly the power fostering the fecundity of women. The Maori, for example, believed that the moon was the permanent husband of all women; and scholars have acknowledged that the 260-day ritual calendar of the Maya of Central America is "directly derived from the experience of human reproduction," i.e., nine lunar revolutions equaling a nine-month gestation period, equalling (approximately) 260 days. In addition, the moon's generative power was also a force that governed the waters of the sea and the cycles of increase and decrease, death and rebirth. Laurens Van Der Post recounts the story of his travels with some African Bushmen. It was night, the Bushmen were up dancing; and when Van Der Post asked them why no one was going to sleep, he was told that they would be dancing all night because the moon was waning and "we must show her how we love her or she won't come back."

Fear and disapproval of the "feminine" power of the moon, however, has manifested itself in many tribal societies where menstruating women are routinely segregated from their villages. The Roman naturalist Pliny stated

English Folklore 13's

In English folklore, the most ominous date for marriage is **Friday, May 13.** But *no* Friday the 13th bodes well for nuptials. As the August 28, 1967, edition of *The Times* of London reported, "When she telephoned to Caxton Hall to inquire what day would not be unduly crowded for a wedding, she was assured the **Friday the 13th** was guaranteed to find the market sluggish."

"Mr. Jack Ellis, mineworker, of Hucknall, Nottinghamshire, who claims he has had three years of bad luck, is to be allowed to change the number of his council house from **13 Arden Close** to 11A." (*The Times* of London, October 23, 1968)

The **Number 13 bus** in London remained unharmed throughout World War II.

Baseball 13's

October 3, 1951: In the deciding third game of the pennant playoffs between the Brooklyn Dodgers and the New York Giants, and with two men on base in the ninth inning, Dodgers pitcher Ralph Branca, wearing the **number 13** on his uniform, threw the ball that Bobby Thompson hit into the stands for a three-run homer, enabling the Giants to win the pennant.

September 5, 1995: Baltimore Orioles shortstop Cal Ripken, Jr., played in his 2,131st consecutive game on September 5, breaking Lou Gehrig's record set in 1933. Ripkin had not missed a game in **13 years.**

that a menstruating woman would destroy crops, sour wines, rust iron, tarnish mirrors, and blunt knives. The Book of Leviticus warns: "And if a woman have an issue, and her issue in her flesh be blood, she shall be put apart seven days. . . . And every thing that she lieth upon in her separation shall be unclean: every thing also that she sitteth upon shall be unclean" (Leviticus 15:19–20). As if to explain these attitudes, Joseph Campbell wrote: "In the older mother myths and rites the light and darker aspects of the mixed thing that is life had been honored equally and together, whereas in the later, male-oriented, patriarchal myths, all that is good and noble was attributed to the new, heroic master gods, leaving to the native nature powers the character only of darkness—to which, also, a negative moral judgment was now added. For, as a great body of evidence shows, the social as well as mythic orders of the two contrasting ways of life were opposed."

But the older mother myths and remembrances of early moon cults have continued to manifest themselves in unlikely places. Consider the famous series of apparitions of the Virgin Mary in Fátima, Portugal, seen by three shepherd children in 1917. A young girl, Lucia dos Santos, and her two cousins reported that on May 13, 1917, they had seen in the Cova da Iria a beautiful lady, surrounded by a dazzling light, who told them that she came from heaven, that they should recite the Rosary every day, and that she would appear on the thirteenth day of the following six months. Our Lady "appeared" on June 13 and on the 13th of the next four months, usually with a flash of light and the sounds of buzzing and thunder, and with either a whirling or a trembling sun, followed by her departure toward the east. On October 13, 1917, about seventy thousand people gathered on a rainy day in anticipation of the Virgin's last visit. It is said that rain clouds parted, and that the sun trembled and danced and whirled like a giant catherine wheel. Thirteen years later, on October 13, 1930, the Bishop of Leiria declared the apparitions at Fátima, along with the Marian sightings at La Salette and Lourdes, to be the most important of the twentieth century until that time.

When I asked several scholars, priests, and Catholic theologians why they thought these serial apparitions at Fátima always occurred on the 13th of the month, none could give me an explanation. A retired theologian from a Catholic university even dismissed my question by remarking that "God acts freely and doesn't need a particular reason to do something on a particular date." In the context of my thinking about the number 13, however, I recalled that the Virgin Mary's link with the moon goddess tradition is clearly reflected in the etymological connection between Maria and the Italian *mare* (sea). The Virgin is known as *Stella Maris* (Star of the Sea). The crescent moon is an attribute of the great goddess Isis, Queen of Heaven, who is described as a ship of light on the sea of night. Even by the Fathers of the Church, Mary was referred to as the Moon of the Church, the Spiritual Moon, the Perfect and Eternal Moon. In medieval art, the Virgin was occasionally represented enthroned on the moon, like Selene, the Greek moon goddess; and in paintings of the Assumption, the crescent moon is often placed under Our Lady's feet. In Revelation, moreover, it is written: "And there appeared a great wonder in heaven; a woman clothed with the sun, and the moon under her feet, and upon her head a crown of twelve stars" (Revelation 12:1).

It is also said that the image of the Black Virgin, as we know it from the statues in shrines at Montserrat, Guadalupe, and many other churches, relates to the realm of the dark moon—the three days of the new moon when it cannot be seen and where light gestates, waiting to be reborn. There are mothers in many parts of the world who still hold their babies up to the new moon, beseeching Mother Moon to increase the stature and strength of their infants and to enable them to continually renew their lives, just as the moon itself does. Was it not therefore possible, I wondered, that the moon and its kindred number, 13, had all that time kept their hidden association with the Virgin-as-moon-goddess alive, which is why Mary "appeared" to the three shepherd children at Fátima on the 13th day of each of those six months in 1917?

In the Syriac text of *The Departure of My Lady from This World* we read: "And the apostles also ordered that there should be a commemoration of the Blessed one on the thirteenth of Ab [August], on account of the vines bearing fruit, that clouds of hail, bearing stones of wrath, might not come, and the trees be broken, and the fruits, and the vines with their clusters." In the case of Fátima, the Virgin Mary supposedly appeared not just to turn aside storms but to announce a message both of Christian redemption and of lunar death and regeneration.

Blame it on the moon, the moon goddess, and the number 13.

A LEGEND OF THE KIOWA PEOPLE, one of the tribes of the Plains Indians, tells of the Thirteen Original Clan Mothers who were the tribe's wisdom keepers. After the destruction of the world by fire, the legend goes, the Clan Mothers assumed human shape, formed a sisterhood, walked the earth, and created thirteen medicine shields, each exemplifying a specific medicine that each of the mothers brought into the world. Then, one day, the Clan Mothers suddenly vanished.

The stories and teachings of this mother clan is part of a lost oral tradition of woman's medicine that stands in contrast to the "male medicine" or "male warrior" way that is prevalent in most Native American communities today. Over the past twenty years, the Thirteen Original Clan Mothers, who are said to be the thirteen healing aspects of the Earth Mother and Grandmother Moon, became the spirit teachers and role models of Jamie Sams. Sams is a Native American medicine teacher of Seneca, Cherokee, and French ancestry. In the 1970s, when she was in her early twenties, Sams journeyed to Mexico where she studied with two Kiowa Grandmothers, Cisi Laughing Crow and Berta Broken Bow, both in their hundreds, who passed down to her the mostly forgotten traditions of the Clan Mothers. In her book *The 13 Original Clan Mothers,* Sams has visualized each of the ancient Clan Mothers, and placed each of their medicine stories on a printed medicine wheel with its Twelve Cycles of Truth and an additional thirteenth Cycle of Truth in the center of the wheel. The names of each of the Clan Mothers is given under each of the thirteen numbers on the Wheel:

According to Jamie Sams, the meaning and function of the Thirteen Clan Mothers are as follows:

1. TALKS WITH RELATIONS (The Mother of Nature/Keeper of Rhythm, Weather, and the Seasons) who teaches us how to Learn the Truth.

2. WISDOM KEEPER (The Protectress of Sacred Traditions) who teaches us how to Honor the Truth.

3. WEIGHS THE TRUTH (The Keeper of Equality and the Guardian of Justice) who teaches us how to Accept the Truth.

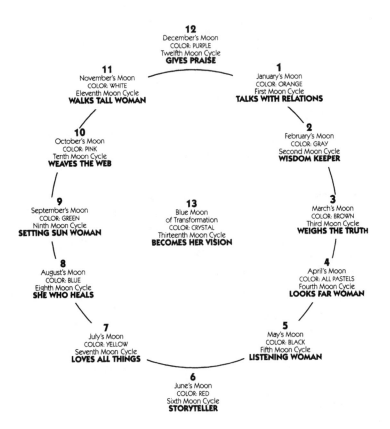

12
December's Moon
COLOR: PURPLE
Twelfth Moon Cycle
GIVES PRAISE

11
November's Moon
COLOR: WHITE
Eleventh Moon Cycle
WALKS TALL WOMAN

1
January's Moon
COLOR: ORANGE
First Moon Cycle
TALKS WITH RELATIONS

10
October's Moon
COLOR: PINK
Tenth Moon Cycle
WEAVES THE WEB

2
February's Moon
COLOR: GRAY
Second Moon Cycle
WISDOM KEEPER

9
September's Moon
COLOR: GREEN
Ninth Moon Cycle
SETTING SUN WOMAN

13
Blue Moon
of Transformation
COLOR: CRYSTAL
Thirteenth Moon Cycle
BECOMES HER VISION

3
March's Moon
COLOR: BROWN
Third Moon Cycle
WEIGHS THE TRUTH

8
August's Moon
COLOR: BLUE
Eighth Moon Cycle
SHE WHO HEALS

4
April's Moon
COLOR: ALL PASTELS
Fourth Moon Cycle
LOOKS FAR WOMAN

7
July's Moon
COLOR: YELLOW
Seventh Moon Cycle
LOVES ALL THINGS

5
May's Moon
COLOR: BLACK
Fifth Moon Cycle
LISTENING WOMAN

6
June's Moon
COLOR: RED
Sixth Moon Cycle
STORYTELLER

The Thirteen Clan Mothers.

4. LOOKS FAR WOMAN (The Seer/Oracle/Dreamer/Prophet) who teaches us how to See the Truth.

5. LISTENING WOMAN (The Mother of Tiyoweh, the Stillness, and Inner Knowing) who teaches us how to Hear the Truth.

6. STORYTELLER (The Guardian of the Medicine Stories) who teaches us how to Speak the Truth.

7. LOVES ALL THINGS (The Mother of Unconditional Love and All Acts of Pleasure) who teaches us how to Love the Truth.

8. SHE WHO HEALS (The Intuitive Healer/Midwife/Herbalist) who teaches us how to Serve the Truth.

9. SETTING SUN WOMAN (The Keeper of Tomorrow's Dreams and Goals) who teaches us how to Live the Truth.

10. WEAVES THE WEB (The Mother of Creativity/the Muse/the Artist) who teaches us how to Work with Truth.

11. WALKS TALL WOMAN (The Guardian of Leadership and the Keeper of New Paths) who teaches us how to Walk the Truth.

12. GIVES PRAISE (The Mother of All Acts of Thanksgiving and Keeper of Abundance) who teaches us how to Be Grateful for the Truth.

13. BECOMES HER VISION (The Guardian of Transformation and Transmutation/The Keeper of the Emergence of Spirit into Physical Form) who teaches us how to Be the Truth.

At her home in Santa Fe, New Mexico, Jamie Sams talked to me about the Clan Mothers and about the shell of Turtle that is supposed to have been Earth Mother's first lunar calendar. "The circle framed in the center of the shell," Sams told me, "has thirteen parts and represents the Thirteen Original Clan Mothers and their guardianship of the thirteen lunar cycles. Every time women would withdraw to have their menses inside the moon lodge, they would mark off one of those shell parts so that they would know that another moon had passed; and when they were all marked off, they would realize that the thirteenth moon had passed and that they

Ramses II's 13th Son

In 1995, archaeologists in Egypt discovered a large tomb in the Valley of Kings near Luxor that they believe is the resting place of most of the 52 sons of Ramses II, whose 66-year reign occurred in the **13th century B.C.** Twelve crown princes died before their father; and Merneptah, **the 13th son** of Ramses' second queen, succeeded his father as pharaoh from 1224–1214 B.C. Many scholars consider Merneptah, and not Ramses, to be the actual pharaoh of the Biblical Exodus.

themselves were due for personal transformation.

"Our lunar calendar consists of twenty-eight days, like a woman's menstrual cycle, and the new moon is never counted because it is void—we call it 'void of the moon.' The new moon, or dark of the moon, is when you want to plant root vegetables, which in the Chinese tradition are *yin,* or female, below the earth, just as a child in the womb is in darkness. Things like tomatoes, eggplant, corn, and squash you want to plant at the full moon because things that grow above the earth are considered *yang,* or male. Root vegetables are planted at the dark of the moon because it takes the magnetic pull of the earth to make carrots, yams, and onions grow well. And we don't count the void of the moon because it represents the zero day."

"So it's like the fertile void," I said.

"Right. The fertile void," Sams replied. "And the zero is never counted in numerology because if you go back to Pythagorean or Tibetan numerology, zero represents wholeness, the pregnant void of that which will be but which is not yet in form."

"I take it you believe that the fear of the number 13 is in a sense the fear of the moon cycle," I remarked.

"The maligning of the number 13 goes back to the rise of the patriarchal religions about sixty thousand years ago," said Sams. "The matriarchal, pagan, earth goddess–based religion was so powerful, and so many men were so frightened of it since they came from a different tradition, that they labeled women as being the embodiment of sin. Mount Sinai basically means "Mother Mountain," and in Genesis the supposed culprit is the feminine [Eve]. So this incredible fear took over, and in Christianity the fear of black magic increased during the time of the Inquisitions, when they burned women who were widowed or childless and labeled them as witches. The original witches' covens occurred when women got together at key points in the fertility cycles—the equinoxes and the solstices. And since women bled thirteen times a year, there were thirteen members, each representing

TURTLE OF THE THIRTEEN MOONS

"The shell of Turtle shows us that the Earth Mother gave us the first lunar calendar. The circle framed in the center of the shell has thirteen parts and is representative of the Thirteen Original Clan Mothers and their guardianship of the thirteen lunar cycles."

—Jamie Sams

one moon cycle of the year, and they celebrated the cycle through dance and with gratitude for all things born of woman. Then, as you read in Eco's *The Name of the Rose,* they came to embody all the frustrations and greatest fears of all of those men living in celibacy, who then wrote down what black magic was supposed to be and what the Evil One and women could do to you."

"What about the notion of 'uncleanliness' with regard to menstruation?" I asked.

"Maybe I ought to go back to plain old everyday physiology," Sams responded. "The cervix is open, and the blood that was used to keep the womb fertile for the previous twenty-eight days, which is now old blood, is released through the opening in the cervix. Well, that old blood was considered tainted or unclean. So when women were having their periods they were segregated by the men of the tribe, who were scared to death of their power during that time. Because through the opening of the cervix women were able to receive into their bodies light, information, clarity, and they would have dreams and visions, scaring people with what they knew. They would have revelations like, 'Gee, Uncle Joe's going to die tomorrow.' And the guy died. So maybe somebody way back then decided that a woman wasn't clean at that time.

"We're brought up to believe all that 'unclean' stuff—it *is* a crummy time, your breasts hurt, you're bloated, you don't take time for yourself. And *that* belief system has created the disease of PMS. I've known women from New York City who have come to me for healing who don't even have a period anymore because they have so bought into the corporate world, and so denied their feminine side, that they've become like men. There's a book called *Sacred Virgin, Holy Whore* that is about the legendary female Pope Joan, who lived during the ninth century. At that time priests could marry; this girl's parents were missionaries and she was raised in this tradition and went all the way up. As soon as she rose to the highest seat of the Roman Catholic Church, her periods totally stopped. She fell in love with a man who was a cardinal, and she got pregnant after her investiture. And the crowd killed her, tore her apart limb from limb. If you look throughout history, you notice that whenever women had some degree of power, it was

The Orient and the Number 13

In China and Japan, it is the number 4, not 13, that is thought of as bad luck. This is because the word for the number 4 in both Chinese and Japanese is a homonym of the word for "death." Today, however, many hotels in Japan omit floors and rooms numbered both 4 *and* 13.

Though they were not carried out, tariffs against thirteen Japanese luxury cars were proposed by the Clinton administration in 1995. The thirteen models, which came to be known as "**The Unlucky 13,**" were:

Acura Legend	Infiniti Q45
Acura 3.2TL	Infiniti J30
Lexus LS400	Infiniti I30
Lexus SC400	Mazda 929
Lexus SC300	Mazda Millennia
Lexus GS300	Mitsubishi Diamante (sedan)
Lexus ES300	

taken away from them, and that the most private aspects of their lives became things to be feared."

"Is this thirteen-moon cycle consciousness respected by any of the Native American tribes today?" I asked.

"In some tribes," Sams replied. "You have patrilineal tribes so frightened of women to this day that if you are in your moon time, they won't let you anywhere near a ceremony. Because during the Trail of Tears in the 1840s, most of the wisdom traditions died when the elders died. So today it's like picking up a piece here, a piece there. The two Kiowa Grandmothers, who were in their hundreds when I studied with them in Mexico in the 1970s, did not go on the Trail of Tears, nor did they or their families accept living on a reservation, and thus they were able to preserve the wisdom of the ancient teachings.

"One of the things that Native American women—at least those who were dreamers—used to do over four hundred years ago was to go out-of-body into dream states and connect with women from other tribes who were also out-of-body; and they would share the same visions, dreams, and stories. There was no language barrier, because when you hear an inner voice it's always in your own language."

"You refer to the thirteenth Clan Mother as Becomes Her Vision. What do you mean by that?" I asked.

"Becomes Her Vision," she replied, "is a present action, it's in the now. In the Seneca tradition we believe that every breath you take is a sacred breath of life because it's the only thing human beings can't live without. The center of your sacred space is in between the in-breath and the out-breath. So if you hold your breath for five seconds, you are then resting in the center of your total self, and all of your gifts, talents, and abilities are available to you in that moment. And your individual rhythm is measured by the beating of your heart with that of the Earth Mother's."

"What does Becomes Her Vision teach us?" I asked.

"That everything and anything can be transformed, nothing is ever written in stone unless you've decided that it is. The moment you decide it's no longer written in stone and that you are going to stretch, you stretch. You can be what you're striving toward, and at that moment you become it.

"The more conscious you are of every act in your life, the more fortuitous and miracle-filled life seems to be. If you are not aware of the beauty of a sunrise, of being grateful for every breath you take into your body, of subtle changes in the weather, or of an animal showing up in an unexpected place that could be a teacher to you, then there *are* no miracles. You think everything is mundane and lackluster. You begin to believe that everything in and about and around you is on a tried-and-true schedule that is completely and totally infiltrated with boredom, because you have not become conscious of how every single act of life can support joy."

"You state that each of the Thirteen Clan Mothers teaches us something," I mentioned. "Together, you say, they teach us how to learn, honor, accept, see, hear, speak, love, serve, live, work with, walk, be grateful for, and be the truth."

"Exactly," she replied. "And how many people can do it? Believe it or not, the most simple people on our planet normally do it without even realizing that they're doing it. I joke that 'In the beginning was the Word, and it was misunderstood.'

"The Maya say, 'I am another one of yourself.' What I want you to realize from the Medicine Wheel of the Thirteen Clan Mothers is that every one of

A Year with 13 Moons

A year with **13 moons** occurs on average every 2.72 years. The thirteenth moon, traditionally called a blue moon, does not have anything to do with the color blue except when atmospheric conditions seem to suggest this coloration. Since 29.53 days pass between full moons, there is almost never a full moon in the month of February. A blue moon occurred in June 1996 (a blue moon in June!); and in 1999 there will be the unusual appearance of two full moons both in January and in March of that year, and none in February. Custom has it that one should make a wish upon the appearance of a blue moon: Remember to make those two extra wishes in 1999. As the new millennium approaches, we will all need them.

those twelve Clan Mothers that came to walk the earth is a part of you, and *you* are the thirteenth, and you are observing every single thing and feeling every single feeling and hearing every single sound and tasting and touching and smelling every single thing that *they* have experienced. *You are Becomes Her Vision.*"

"Someone suffering from triskaidekaphobia," I say, "might pass out if they read your book."

"Or the phobia would disappear," she told me. "Because they would understand where their fear came from. I mean, this isn't Father Earth! They decolonized Mars a long time ago. Everything is born of a woman. . . . Only the seahorse and the earthworm are androgynous and weren't born strictly from the female of the species. Which kind of tells us where we've been, since those two creatures might possibly be remnants of an ancient past. Plato's right: We're split apart, but it wasn't always that way."

"Thirteen is the vision of the Clan Mothers," I said to Jamie Sams. "What does the number 13 ultimately mean to you?"

"Thirteen," she said, "is every single time people come to a crossroads in their lives and feel that they have enough of the inner strength that they require to step out into the world—outside of their inner world—as healed and transformed humans, to share it with all of us."

A CHILD'S THIRTEENTH YEAR, the first of teenage existence, is traditionally the beginning of adolescence. It is a time when biology has laid the groundwork for sudden reproductive fertility, and for a change in the child's cognitive structure, affect, and behavior. Along with all this is the conflict between a child's building a sense of self, in accord with his or her

Puberty by Edvard Munch.

needs and feelings, and the more confining demands of the adult world. In the West, particularly in the twentieth century, the celebration of an autonomous belief system has encouraged children to "do their own thing." In the words of a fourteen-year-old American girl, "Before, I didn't know what I was doing, and now I feel that what I am doing is my own." In traditional societies, however, the terms of maturity are yoked to an acceptance of the values of the adult community. "At thirteen," Jamie Sams says, "Native American children let go of the infant-and-child stage and begin training to become full-fledged working members of the tribe." Or, as Professor Pierre Erny comments about black African children, "Since initiation is entry into the society, the child must learn and interiorize without equivocation certain necessities of collective life: courage, work, moral and physical strength, resistance, passive obedience, solidarity, conformity, earning a living, keeping a secret."

What is it like to be a thirteen-year-old American girl? There are at least three ways to find out: be one, ask one, or inquire of someone who used to be one. I asked a writer from northern California named C. B. Parrish, now in her early forties, and this is what she reported:

> Petrified that my little sister, just turned twelve, the sensible one, had not only beat me to it, but somehow in her speed prevented me *ever* bemoaning The Curse, like the big girls do, I turned tomboy for good. Surfer shirts, faded blue jeans, desert boots, strawberry hair pixie-cut, freckles full-blasted off my every inch, knocking you back a piece. I broke the stride of that cantankerous old bag who ran the stables, *just* by turning around. "Young man! You get off that horse before I knock you off! Oh! Uh. You're a girl! Good Christ, yes you are!" Boys yibbered "Camel" at me, goosing me in school, yelling "That's not a bra! It's two pup tents sewn together." My sensible little, big, sister never got those! First *or* second.
>
> Between birthday thirteen and the next was my last full year with Martin Luther King Jr. alive out there. Was sure The False—shooting, hosing, bomb-

ing—laboring to become The True just could not work, but then I still thought I was half-Dutch, half-Portuguese, too. Didn't know yet my gramma was full Cherokee, had lied to marry herself off the reservation. Didn't know my mother could *still* be so scared about Hitler and McCarthy she'd drop half her genes, burn my essays on world harmony behind my back. Never got a bit of this stupid kicking for "safety" over stuff as impossible to credit as racism, xenophobia. Just could not feature the hate; but the big *news,* from my patronizing drunk uncle with the poking mustache puckered to birthday me up one side and down the other—that thirteen is an unlucky number—did seem particularly germane. Like a hawk zeroed-in on a screaming rodent so intently he splats against a barn, I'd watch every minute of Fridays the 13th. Watched them so hard I splatted on the next day.

My horse was named Angel. Short for Hell's Angel. Jumped over buildings if you pointed her there. Raced smarty boys on quarter horses, and beat them all. I was in school or I was on Angel. Period. Period. Saturday the 14th of May, in a sucking flash that left Right Now scrambling in midair for its minute back, the cold maw of death yanked me off my saddle to the dirt. Angel stood over me, reins flapping in all directions, agape, agog for help. Angel! I'm dying. Someone's mother hauled me up and drove me home. "You are not dying. You'll definitely live. Go in and go to bed. Wait till your mother gets home." Writhing on my bed, chanting death, death, death, I passed out. I next awakened bloody to the stultifying news that this stark-raving imminence of death was my future, and officially All In My Head.

Eight months later, Saturday the 14th of January, Angel kicked me in the head, all accidentally, sending me in a fabulous arc into the salt lick ten feet away. Got up and flew in through the barn window, landing in a sweet blend of dust and dry horse manure. My sister found me, head gushing and clutching a perfectly-round well-salted scrape on my elbow. She went dead white: "Believe me, you can forget your elbow, and you can't fly." At the hospital, a scarlet creek trickled from between my toes, heading down the corridor after a formerly healthy little old lady being carted off from the sight of me. Insisting to my father I *could* fly, not only this time but before too, I watched the old lady's shoes receding down the hall on a gurney just ahead of my creek. I must have leaked all my flight down that creek because I never flew awake from that day.

Not so young as to spend evenings prattling on the phone with my girl-friend as Mrs. Lennon to Mrs. McCartney anymore, I was crazy for Humphrey Bogart. I do love *intense* men. Mapped myself the only possible husband, and nope, not your usual specs by any stretch. Never a paycheck wimp, or inclined to deal with stupidity—or (ack! phooey!) "acceptability"—he'd be strong. He'd work this world with no seam between doer and done. An artist/out-doorsman, he'd spend long spells away, but when we were with each other, we'd *be* each other. We would *not* be playing at ourselves.

Thirty years has stretched from then till now. The truest thing I can say about thirteen is: I was absolutely right then. Reality broke over a pristine shore. Nothing has put the lie to it in all my years. I will live up to it. I will fly again.

In many parts of the world, there are still places where thirteen-year-olds undergo some kind of rite of passage. In the traditional Jewish bar mitzvah, one comes upon a possibly unique rite of passage that requires, not an act or initiation involving physical pain or endurance, but rather an act of literacy—the reading of a passage from the Torah.

Lawrence Kushner, rabbi of Congregation Beth El in Sudbury, Massachusetts, is the author of a number of remarkable books on Jewish mysticism. When I asked him about the practice and function of a bar mitzvah, I mentioned that I had been told it is not really correct to speak of "being" bar mitzvahed or of "having" a bar mitzvah, since the term "bar mitzvah," which comes from the Aramaic, is not really a verb or a noun.

"That's true," Rabbi Kushner replied. "One *becomes* a son or daughter of the commandment. At a certain point you're considered to be religiously mature and responsible for the commandments you fulfill or don't fulfill; you're no longer your parents' problem. At the bar or bat mitzvah, the par-ents actually recite a little formula that says, 'Thank God for removing this burden from us now.' So you can't blame your parents anymore.

"Reading from the Torah is a celebration of the state you've entered simply by virtue of being thirteen years old. (A girl can celebrate her bat mitzvah at twelve years old.) When you become sexually mature you are religiously obligated to follow the commandments on your own. And if you want to hear something heavy about 13, here it is: After you've been on the planet for thirteen rotations of the sun, most people grow two pubic hairs. They can get pregnant or impregnate someone. In fact there's a rabbinic tradition that says that the indication of puberty is the appearance of two pubic hairs. Isn't it funny that 13 coincides with sexual maturity?

"Jewish tradition certainly was on the right track when it affirmed that at thirteen years old one had the plumbing to 'do it' and that therefore one *should* do it, leave home, and earn a liv-

12 + 1

Zeus and the 12 gods of Olympus

Jacob and 12 sons

Odysseus and his 12 companions contesting with the Cyclops Polyphemus

Romulus and the 12 shepherds

Balder and the 12 judges

King Arthur and the 12 Knights of the Round Table

The Norman pirate-chieftain Rollo and his 12 warriors

Roland and the 12 Peers of France

The sun at its zenith surrounded by the 12 signs of the zodiac

A judge and the 12 members of the jury

A Catharist cell

A witches' coven

A baker's dozen

ing, take a spouse. What we do now is keep young people in a state of ado-lescence that didn't really exist until about 150 years ago. It's obvious and natural that people used to marry 'young'; my grandfather married at sev-enteen. It's much healthier than joining a fraternity and carrying on like an idiot. Some future historian looking back is going to say, 'These kids were really screwed up. They couldn't get married and make a home and do what physiologically they were supposed to do.' A thirteen-year-old should be able to make a home and do what his body has prepared him to do. So-ciety won't allow a kid to earn a living and be a mensch and support a fam-ily. My theory is that we don't let kids get married earlier because we want to keep them out of the labor pool. So we've invented graduate school."

"You sound a bit old-fashioned about this," I said.

"I'm a Neanderthal!" Rabbi Kushner replied.

"Do you think biology is destiny?" I asked him.

"No, it's just that society denies biology at its own peril. Witness the state of affairs we're in now. I think it was healthier when kids who were thirteen, fourteen, fifteen years old got married and had children. In that way, people could live to become great-grandparents, too. What we have now is a situation in which children get married at the age of thirty-seven, say, and the chance that their kids will have an opportunity to know their grandparents is very slim. And what happens in the American Jewish com-munity is that bar mitzvahs have become like weddings."

"What do you mean?" I asked.

"I mean that virtually every social obligation that used to apply to wed-dings now applies to bar mitzvahs. People are afraid that their parents won't be alive by the time their grandchildren get married. So a bar mitzvah be-comes a weekend event, people come in from all over the country, parents spend twenty thousand dollars—all the things they used to do for wed-dings. And now when a couple gets married it's rare that there are any grandparents left at all."

"Would you really marry a thirteen-year-old boy and a twelve-year-old girl?" I asked Rabbi Kushner.

"Unfortunately," he said, "in today's society this would be a sign of major dysfunction in the family."

I next asked the rabbi about the Thirteen Principles of Jewish Faith, which were formulated in the twelfth century by the great Jewish philosopher Moses Maimonides. "It was fashionable in Maimonides' time, especially under the influence of Christianity, to come up with a list of what you should believe," Rabbi Kushner told me. "And so Maimonides, being the smartest Jew who ever was, said, 'I'll try to come up with a list of things every Jew should believe.' Unfortunately, in the Jewish community he couldn't find more than five Jews who agreed with any three of these principles. So they never caught on. But they made a song out of them—they were sung as part of the morning liturgy—called the *Yigdal,* and you can still hear it sung in synagogues around the world."

"What are the Thirteen Principles?" I asked.

"I'll give you a very loose translation of them," said Rabbi Kushner:

1. There is a God.
2. There's only one.
3. He ain't got a body.
4. God was the first and the last beyond time.
5. God's the only one worth talking to.
6. It's possible for God to get through to people (i.e., prophecy).
7. Moses was the clearest prophet there ever was.
8. The Torah is an accurate representation of what God wants.
9. The Torah isn't going to change.
10. He knows if you've been bad or good, so be good for goodness' sake.
11. He pays bad people back and rewards good people.
12. He's gonna send the Messiah.
13. He's gonna resurrect the dead.

Lucky 13

On July 16, 1933, the steamer *S.S. Chelyuskin* departed from Leningrad on a historic polar expedition across the Northeast Passage to study the Soviet Arctic. On its way to Vladivostok, the vessel was caught in ice floes and gradually drifted toward the northwest. On **February 13,** 1934, the *Chelyuskin,* crushed by ice, finally sank. All but one of the 105 people aboard disembarked safely onto the ice floes with enough food, supplies, and equipment to enable everyone to live on the ice and carry on the expedition's scientific work. An enormous rescue expedition with airplanes, icebreakers, and dog teams was organized immediately, and Russian radio aviators transmitted periodic reports on the rescue operation, which was called "one of the greatest and most epic in the history of Arctic exploration." All members of the *Chelyuskin* crew were finally reached and saved on **April 13,** 1934.

"The thirteenth principle sounds a bit controversial," I suggested.

"Everything is controversial to Jews. You know in the old days when your grandmother died and was buried," the rabbi said, "they'd put a little bit of earth from the Holy Land in a bag and place it in the coffin with her because she wanted to be resurrected in the Holy Land, and she believed that the earth was like a homing device that would help her come up in the middle of Jerusalem.

"But I think that principle number 3 is Judaism's great gift to world religion—the principle that God doesn't have a body. There's nothing to see. God doesn't look like anything. God's right here right now, and it's not that

On **October 13,** 1983, **13 passengers** (1 child and 12 adults, including the pilot who was celebrating his birthday on that day) boarded an Aeroflot helicopter **(tail number: 14013)** in Vladivostok en route to Yekinka. In the waters off the coast of Dal'negorsk the copter rescued a drowning Japanese sailor and flew him to a hospital. The next day the passengers again boarded the helicopter, which started to take off, when suddenly the engine failed and the copter crashed into a garden, breaking its nose and tail. Fortunately, there was no fire and only one minor injury. According to one of the passengers, Alexei Gurko, who is presently Aeroflot's station manager at Dulles International Airport, "As far as I'm concerned, **13,** for me, is now a lucky number. Believe me! And I'm glad to say that Aeroflot planes *do* have a **row 13**—some other airlines' planes do not—and there's more leg room in **row 13.** When I first moved to the United States and noticed that there wasn't a **13th floor** in my apartment building, I couldn't believe it. People would be much happier if they had a floor 13; they don't know what they're missing!"

you can't see Him because He's invisible but that there's nothing to see. I think that's a religiously very daring and extraordinary insight."

"Yet principle number 13 asserts that the dead will be resurrected in bodily form," I mentioned.

"Yes," the rabbi responded, "our bodies are OK, God gave us bodies for reasons we don't understand. He didn't give us the bodies that we think we should have gotten. I think I should have been the opening quarterback for the Miami Dolphins, but I wasn't. I got to be a rabbi in Sudbury, Massachusetts."

"What do you think of numerology in Judaism?" I asked him.

The 13 Man

When the French film director Claude Lelouch *(A Man and a Woman, And Now My Love)* created his production company in 1960, he originally thought of calling it Apocalypse Films. His lawyer, however, thought it a terrible name for a company. At a meeting with the director, he asked Lelouch if he was superstitious. "No," Lelouch replied. "Well," said the lawyer, "today is the **13th of March,** it's now precisely **13 hours** (1 P.M.), and your name has **13 letters** in it." At that moment, the company **Film 13** was born.

When Lelouch goes to a hotel and **room 13** is available, he requests it. At the theater he'll ask for **seat number 13.** When he built a racing boat he baptized it **Friday the 13th.** His company's screening room is called **Club 13,** and he owns a hotel in Deauville called **Club 13 Normandie.** The office address of Film 13 is 15, Avenue Hoche, but

"Some lady once came up to me at a lecture in Ventura, California," Rabbi Kushner replied, "and said to me, 'I came here on bus number 23, what does that mean?' And I said, 'It must mean that you should go home on bus number 23.'

"In general, I'm not aware of there being any problem with the number 13 in Judaism. It's an important number, and all the associations I have with it are positive, like the stars in Joseph's dream."

RABBI KUSHNER HAD TOLD ME that there was a rich tradition concerning the number 13 in Judaism, and he suggested I speak to an au-

when Lelouch tried to change it officially to **13 Avenue Hoche**, he was unfortunately unable to do so.

"It has nothing to do with the significance or symbolism of the number," says Arlette Gordon, Lelouch's casting director and head of public relations for Film 13. "It's just an instinct, a feeling. He once met Edith Piaf on the street: she was waiting in a taxicab while her nurse was doing some shopping for her at Gallerie Lafayette. Claude approached the car, opened the door, and said, 'I admire you so much, may I talk to you?' And she said OK and invited him inside. That meeting took place on **the 13th of the month.**

"Claude loves making decisions on the 13th, but he doesn't wait or look for that date. He once said, 'I don't *believe*, I'm amazed!' I remember his being amazed when he suddenly realized that there were **13 letters** in the title of his most recent film, *Les Misérables*.

"He wears **13 little jewels** in his hat when he shoots."

thority on the body of Jewish mystical teachings called the Kabbalah. Eventually I found my way to Professor Elliot Wolfson, who teaches courses on Jewish mysticism (including Lurianic Kabbalism) at New York University; and it was he who helped guide me through this fascinating but sometimes perplexing material.

In the Jewish Passover Haggadah, there is a famous recitation that concludes, "Who knoweth thirteen? I, saith Israel, know thirteen: There are thirteen divine attributes, twelve tribes, eleven stars, ten commandments . . . ," etc. I asked Professor Wolfson about the thirteen divine attributes (often referred to as the Thirteen Attributes of God's Mercy).

"The Thirteen Attributes," he told me, "is a rabbinic idea that is greatly elaborated in the Kabbalistic tradition, but it's also expressed in Talmudic Judaism. The Thirteen Attributes *(midot)* are first mentioned in Exodus 34:6, and they occur in the context of a discussion between Moses and God when Moses is requesting God's forgiveness of Israel: 'The Lord, The Lord, a God compassionate and gracious, slow to anger, abounding in kindness and faithfulness, extending kindness to the thousandth generation, forgiving iniquity, transgression, and sin.' Now, the rabbis originally had the concept of the Thirteen Attributes and linked it to this biblical text. I don't know where the rabbis were actually getting this doctrine, and I don't think anyone really does. But once it's in place, it's then further developed by Kabbalists.

"Then, of course, there's Jacob and his twelve sons, which is probably the prototype for Jesus and his twelve disciples. That's an obvious thirteen configuration, but I don't remember the Bible making much about the number 13 in that particular case. Later on, though, the Kabbalists do make a big deal about Jacob and his sons, who collectively comprise the entity of Israel; and they state that numerologically the Hebrew word for 'one,' *Ehad,* is equivalent to the numbers 1 + 8 + 4, which equals 13, since *Ehad* consists of the *Aleph* (1), the *Het* (8), and the *Dalet* (4). So there is this notion that the oneness of God and the oneness of the Jewish people is expressed through 13. Thirteen is the fullest expression of the One. And Israel is most truly represented in the power of 13."

"Do you think that the formulation 12 + 1 (God) suggests something about the divine mystery as well?" I asked.

"In the Kabbalah there's no question about it," Professor Wolfson replied. "In the *Sephirot* [ten emanations that comprise a bridge connecting the finite universe with the infinite God], the uppermost aspect of the divine and the first of these emanations *(Keter)* is expressed in terms of thirteen powers. Again, this is a Kabbalistic application of the rabbinic idea of the Thirteen Attributes of God's Mercy we spoke about before. *Keter* is called the world of mercy, it represents pure divine mercy, which for the Kabbalists is the characteristic of beneficence and overflowingness; and *Keter* represents in the fullest and most perfect way this quality of God.

"So you have this idea that within *Keter* there are thirteen potencies or thirteen powers. The *Zohar* (Book of Splendor), written in thirteenth-century Spain, refers to the thirteen curls of the Holy Beard of the Divine. It's essentially the same thing, just a different way of expressing it. *Keter* is sometimes personified as the Holy Ancient One, and you have a description of its beard which is said to contain those thirteen curls. This is just an intensely anthropomorphic way of expressing the idea that what's in this first emanation of the Divine, which is pure mercy, are these thirteen attributes of mercy. And the image of the curls of the beard is that they are like channels through which the overflow comes down."

"The people who conceived of this were certainly very far out," I remarked.

"I've been studying this for a very long time," Professor Wolfson said, "and I am still blown away almost daily by the realization that in the heart of rabbinic Judaism this could have emerged. The energies that were unleashed are quite astonishing. A large part of my research has been to argue that underlying these theosophies is a deeply experiential element. So by studying this you're kind of translated into a different world, a different plane of being."

"In the *Zohar*," I said, "we read about the thirteen-petaled rose. What is that?"

"In the *Zohar,* this is a description of the community of Israel as a mystical symbol that stands for the *Shekinah,* the divine presence. The *Zohar* describes the *Shekinah*—the tenth emanation of the *Sephirot*—as a thirteen-petaled rose. 'Just as the rose has thirteen petals, so the community of Israel has thirteen attributes of mercy that surround it from every side.' The divine presence, which is symbolized both as the rose and the community of

From the 13th Chapter of Apocalypse (The Beast and the AntiChrist)

And I stood upon the sand of the sea, and saw a beast rise up out of the sea, having seven heads and ten horns, and upon his horns ten crowns, and upon his heads the name of blasphemy. . . .

And I saw one of his heads as it were wounded to death; and his deadly wound was healed: and all the world wondered after the beast. . . .

And he opened his mouth in blasphemy against God, to blaspheme his name, and his tabernacle, and them that dwell in heaven. . . .

Here is wisdom. Let him that hath understanding count the number of the beast: for it is the number of a man; and his number is Six hundred threescore and six.

Israel, is surrounded by thirteen attributes of mercy. Obviously, these are not the Thirteen Attributes of which we spoke before, which were in *Keter,* because we're now at a lower stage. But what is very common in Kabbalistic symbolism is that there is a repetition of structures on different levels. So here's the interesting thing: *Keter* is the first of the emanations, which is depicted as comprising thirteen powers . . . and the last of the emanations is depicted as being surrounded by the thirteen attributes of mercy. So there's a perfect parallelism in the structure."

"Which seems to return us to the biblical Thirteen Attributes," I said.

"Yes. You can look upon all of this as a kind of deep meditation on the biblical notion, especially as it's reflected through the prism of the rabbis. The notion of the Thirteen Attributes of Mercy is a leitmotif that's essential to the High Holy Days, when the world, according to the rabbis, is standing under judgment, and the traditional liturgy constantly invokes those thirteen attributes. According to Jewish tradition, the world wouldn't be able to endure if not for God's mercy. What you find in the Kabbalah is a hypermystical application of this idea. But in its basic element it's already present in the rabbinic theology."

"The number 13 is extraordinarily auspicious and numinous in the Kabbalah," I said. "But what about the Book of Esther, in which the King of Persia called together his scribes on the thirteenth day of the first month and announced that every Jew in his kingdom would be killed on the thirteenth day of the twelfth month?"

"But look what happened," Professor Wolfson replied. "The Jews turned the tables on Ahasuerus and were *saved* on the 13th. In the Jewish tradition, especially in the Kabbalistic tradition, you have a total reversal of the notion of 13 as an unlucky number. Even the thirteenth letter in the Hebrew (and the English) alphabet, *Mem* (M), is equivalent to the number 40, which is a number that suggests the idea of resurrection, revival, or renewal— think of the forty days of the flood or the forty days that Moses spent on Mount Sinai. It's really fascinating, the extent to which the number 13 is so sacred."

"THE NUMBER 13 APPEARS EVERYWHERE," Bob Frissell said to me when I met him in Berkeley, California. Frissell, a rebirther and mathematician, is the author of the cult New Age bestseller *Nothing in This Book Is True, But It's Exactly How Things Are,* one of the most curious, bizarre, and confounding books I'd come across in my journey into the realm of the number 13, dealing as it does with sacred geometry, the Great Pyramid, gray aliens, free energy, crop circles, and secret colonies on Mars. In his book Frissell acknowledges his debt to the work and teachings of his witness-guide, Drunvalo Melchizedek, who lives in Wimberly, Texas, and who claims to be nothing less than a "walk-in" from the thirteenth dimension. (Drunvalo, it has been said, "has managed to move through all of the dimensional levels and remain conscious.") I sagely decided to focus my attention on Frissell's intriguing discussion of sacred geometry and the number 13 ("Sacred geometry," the author told me, "is not just lines on a page; rather, it is the sacred motions of Spirit in the Void"), and he elaborated on this at our meeting.

"Genetically speaking," Frissell began, "13 is a very significant number in regard to how the universe is put together. The universe keeps repeating itself, just as octaves on a keyboard keep repeating themselves. So basically what you have is twelve major universes in each octave, with twelve overtones in between. And, as on a piano, there are five black keys, seven white, and the thirteenth is the return. We're living in the third universe—more specifically, in the third dimension—but each one of those other universes is a separate universe as vast as this one. As you go up, the wavelength gets shorter. And in our third dimension we're so veiled that we don't have conscious recall of how to tune into any of these other universes."

"What is the importance of sacred geometry in this context?" I asked.

"The whole idea of the sacred geometry here is the special movement that you and I and all of us made in order to get out of the great Void. Between each one of these dimensional levels, there's a voidness; so you have to know how to move in a very specific way in order to end up here, in our case in a third dimensional level on planet earth.

"The more you look at the sacred geometry, the more it shows you, step by step, that there is a common thread that runs through everything. Think of the first three verses from the opening of Genesis: 'In the beginning God created the heaven and the earth. And the earth was without form, and void; and darkness was upon the face of the deep. And the Spirit of God moved upon the face of the waters. And God said, Let there be light; and there was light.' What is described here is Spirit in the great Void, in the middle of nothingness. And now Spirit in nothingness is going to move in a very specific way in order to create this reality. Figure 1 is showing you geometrically how Spirit is moving. Since you're in total nothingness, you can't move unless you have some parameters. If there's you and nothing else, how would you know if you moved? So what we're doing here is creating a possibility of movement. And the way we're taught to do that is quite simple. Imagine you're in a pitch black room, and though you can't see anything, you're going to project a certain amount of distance ahead of you. And although you know nothing is there, you can do this in four directions—frontward, backward, up, and down. That's what Figure 1 is representing.

"So, from the projection, the next idea is to make a square around you (Figure 2), and from there to form a pyramid (Figure 3). Then bring the lines down to form a pyramid below so that you get an octahedron (Figure 4). (Even though this is only a mental image, it makes movement possible, because now you have a frame of reference.) The next idea is to get from the octahedron to a sphere (Figure 5). And you can do that just by rotating your axis in all the different possible directions.

"In sacred geometry, a straight line is considered male and a curved line female. So by rotating the octahedron on its axis, Spirit went from being

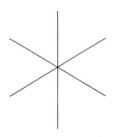

Figure 1

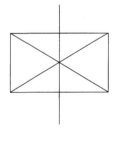

Figure 2

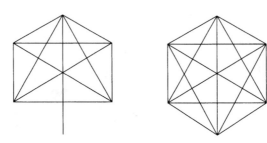

Figure 3   Figure 4

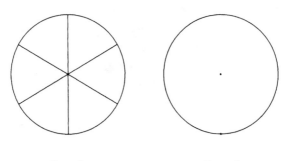

Figure 5   Figure 6

male to being female, i.e., a sphere. The Bible reports that the male was completed first and the female second. This is a movement from straight lines to curved lines. The reason Spirit went from straight lines to curved lines is that the geometric progression necessary for creation is much easier from the female curved lines. Here, Spirit finds itself inside the sphere. Genesis says, 'The Spirit of God moved upon the face of the waters,' but where to? In the entire universe there was only one new place and that was the surface. So Spirit moved to the surface.

"Every motion from then on indicates exactly where to make the following motion until the entire universe is created. Spirit knows what it has to do, which is to create more spheres. What you first have is a *vesica piscis,* or two interlocked spheres, which is the metaphysical structure behind light: 'And God said, Let there be light; and there was light.' So this is the first day of Genesis (Figure 7). Then, by making another sphere, you get the next image, which makes the second day of Genesis (Figure 8). And the rest is automatic (Figures 9–12).

"After the sixth day, you've got the minimum amount of information necessary to give you the entire pattern of the flower of life, which consists of nineteen circles contained within a larger circle. It's the image by means of which everything is created (Figure 13). And if you take one half the radius of the center circle, draw a new circle using the one-half radius, and

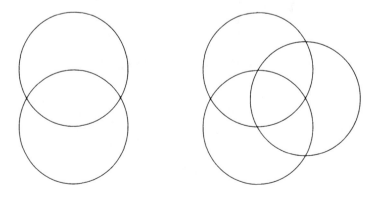

Figure 7   Figure 8

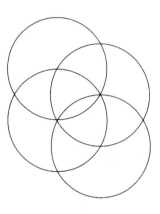

Figure 9

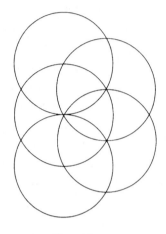

Figure 10

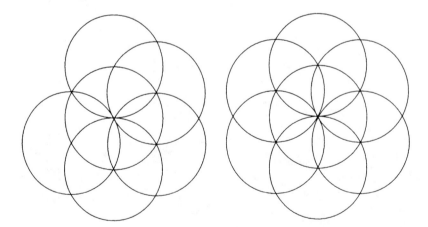

Figure 11

Figure 12

Figure 13

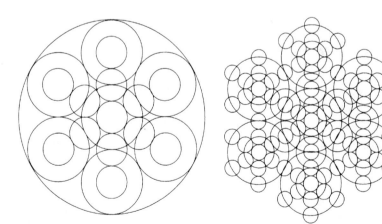

Figure 14   *Figure 15*

then run the circles down the three axes, you will get the fruit of life (Figure 14). Do this one more time and you end up with thirteen circles connected to thirteen circles, or the fruit of life connected to the fruit of life. You can keep doing this operation forever; like the logarithmic spiral, this is a primary geometrical pattern of the universe (Figure 15).

"As I say in my book, the fruit of life with its thirteen circles is a very special, very sacred figure. Thirteen systems of information come out of the fruit of life, and these systems describe in detail every single aspect of our reality, everything that we can think of, see, taste, or smell, right down to the actual atomic structure. The whole process I've been describing here is the map of the movement of Spirit out of nothingness into the creation of the entire reality. It allows us to begin to see logically the unified thread that moves through everything—you, me, everyone, without exception."

ON AUGUST 16 AND 17, 1987, more than the hoped-for 144,000 people gathered at sacred sites and "power points" around the world—Machu Picchu in Peru, the Great Pyramids in Egypt, Mount Fuji in Japan, Mount Shasta in California, and Central Park in New York City—as part of a geomantic Harmonic Convergence. On the morning of August 16, people rose at dawn, established conscious connection with the earth, "resonated in harmony" in order to ward off twenty-five years of catastrophe, chanted, danced, and participated in one of the largest New Age ceremonies of our time.

The theoretician and progenitor of the Harmonic Convergence was José Argüelles—a self-styled visionary, historian, educator, artist, philosopher, and cosmic harmonist—who conceived of this event in 1983 as he drove on Wilshire Boulevard in Los Angeles, where he had a "sudden vision of a type of Earth surrender ritual taking place all over the world." Shortly before the Harmonic Convergence occurred, Argüelles commented: "We hu-

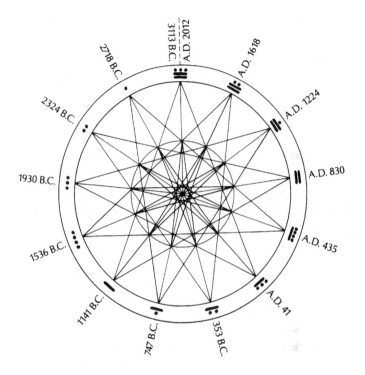

The Great Cycle of Thirteen *baktuns*.

mans provide the nervous system of this organism, earth, and right now the earth is saying, 'Hey! The way things are going, I'm a nervous wreck. Do something different! Nothing else has worked thus far in solving the problems of militarism, environmental pollution, and social discontent, so why not give art, artists, and the creative spirit a try?' "

Argüelles, who is best known for his controversial work on the Maya of Central America, believes that the ancient sacred Mayan calendar reveals a

Great Cycle, and many subcycles, running from 3113 B.C. to A.D. 2012. He describes the Great Cycle in his book *The Mayan Factor* as a "galactic beam of intelligent cultural evolution, 5,125 years in diameter," which "comprises recorded history as we know it." Interestingly, the date 5125 B.C. is written in Mayan chronology as 13.0.0.0.0, a date that will occur again at the end of this Great Cycle on December 21, 2012. When it does, according to Argüelles, the earth will shoot out of the beam and into a "galactic synchronization phase" resulting in a unified planetary and universal telepathic consciousness. Thus, according to Argüelles, the year A.D. 2013 would be the Omega Point in the actual evolutionary completion cycle of the earth. The Harmonic Convergence, he stated, would announce the forthcoming end of the 394-year *baktun* (cycle) designated by the Mayan sacred calendar as *13 Ahau*—"thirteen . . . the most exalted number," Argüelles affirmed, "representative of the dynamic of movement present in everything and by which everything is ever-changing, the sign of Solar Mystery."

To reinforce his call for participants in the event, Argüelles calculated from ancient Aztec calendars that their thirteen cycles of heaven and nine cycles of hell would end on August 16, 1987; and he further pointed to a Hopi legend promising that 144,000 "enlightened teachers" would awaken the rest of humanity on that same day. Moreover, Argüelles noted that it would be the first time in 23,412 years that seven of the nine planets would be situated within 123 degrees of one another, an arrangement known as a grand trine. What more could anyone have wanted? And indeed, although Argüelles had requested 144,000 participants to attend the Harmonic Convergence, more than twice as many people around the world answered the call.

Born of Mexican-American ancestry, José Argüelles was brought up in the United States and returned to Mexico at the age of thirteen. He was inexorably drawn to the Mayan pyramids and the sacred pictorial-numerical

Tzolkin as the harmonic module.

Mayan calendar called the *Tzolkin*. This is the ritual and divinatory calendar, or Count of Days, consisting of a permuting cycle of thirteen numbers and twenty named days—a 13 × 20 matrix that Argüelles refers to as a "harmonic module" and a "periodic table of galactic frequencies." As the author states, "Only 13 numbers are necessary to describe the entire complex we call galactic being—13 numbers each occupying a possibility of 20 positional places for a total of 260 permutations."

In the second chapter of *The Mayan Factor,* Argüelles lets it be known that in his opinion, the Maya, together with their "system," were of galactic origins. The Maya, according to Argüelles, were originally not human beings but rather "galactic agents," extraterrestrial engineers who, with a disarmingly simple and flexible number system, came to our planet to make sure that "the galactic harmonic pattern, not perceivable as yet to our evolutionary position in the galaxy, had been presented and recorded." After "seeding" the earth with this information, declares Argüelles, these agents departed at the end of the ninth *baktun,* enclosed in luminous galactic cocoons. "Despite this coming time of darkness," writes the author, "in which . . . the memory of the galactic masters would be viewed as a childish dream, the numbers of destiny would remain—the 13 numbers and the 20 signs."

If one suspends disbelief and takes Argüelles's sci-fi fantasies as resonant metaphors, one finds frequently illuminating descriptions of such things as the Sacred Calendar (the *Tzolkin*). In Argüelles's words, "If the thirteen numbers are the light that arouses the mind and body, then the twenty directional positions are the water that nourishes this very same mind and body. In the interplay of thirteen numbers and twenty symbols lies the indwelling galactic code-bank that informs the resonant structures comprising the symbol-woven tapestry of our reality."

For the past few years, José Argüelles and his wife, Lloydine, have been traveling widely as "galactic gypsies" in places like Central and South America,

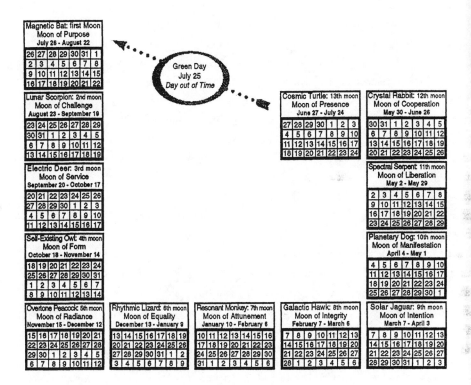

A thirteen-moon calendar: 13 perfect moons of 18 days each; 4 phases of the moon, 4 perfect weeks of 7 days to every moon; 52 perfect weeks, 364 days, plus a day out of time (July 25) every year. *Calendar by John-Erik Omland.*

South Africa, Egypt, India, and Russia. Their mission has been to fulfill what they take to be a Mayan prophecy that requires 144,000 people to reject the "incorrect Gregorian 12-month calendar and the 60-minute hour, neither of which corresponds to any natural cycle." In their place, the Argüelles are promoting the acceptance and adoption of the "correct" 13-month, 28-day calendar that is based on the natural, solar, galactic timing frequency of 13:20 ("13 galactic tones or moons, 20 solar frequencies of fingers-and-toes").

"We have now been living seven years according to 13:20," Argüelles reports, "five years without a belief in money. We have observed that humans are the only species who have to pay for birth, pay for food and shelter, pay for pleasure, and pay for death. And the more we pay, the more we become encumbered in a world of machines, overpopulation, and inflexible laws. And when we ask who is destroying the biosphere, is it the crocodiles, is it the ants, is it the cats and dogs? No. It is we humans. . . . We have observed that the 12:60 world has no Emergency Exit. If you do not, or cannot, pay, you are a criminal, and the police and the bankers are always right. This is all the result of the Time Wars."

In the past, Argüelles specified the dates July 26, 1994, and July 25, 1995, as the last days for "leaving the old time and entering the new time," or else "species-wide destruction" would, he warned, according to the Mayan prophecy, occur within the following five years. Those dates in July have come and gone, and as far as I can tell, there has been no groundswell to overturn the calendar that was imposed on us by priests and political leaders in Babylonia some five thousand years ago.

Many times have I tried to get in touch with José Argüelles in order to ask him about the possible impending destruction of the world, but he has always been one step ahead of me. His associate in northern California, Elizabeth Whitney, however, has tried to explain the nature of this Mayan prophecy to me. "I believe this prophecy is describing a sequence that is in place," she said. "But this is not the Old Testament, it's the *next* testament, and there isn't that emotion-based, fear-mongering, end-of-the-world attitude that people with a limited view of these things tend to exhibit— though wouldn't *you* like the *misguided* world to end?

"It's really more like running a relay race; everytime you get to a certain point, you pass the baton, and that's a significant shift. I don't think it's possible to do a head count with regard to the adoption of the 13:20 calendar. José goes around the world, and his message is received by thousands of

Lloydine Argüelles setting fire to a traditional Gregorian calendar while José Argüelles holds up a thirteen-moon calendar.

people in South America and Japan. It's not like links in a chain, it's exponential or like fireworks. Each second the fireworks are ten times greater than what you saw before. The moment that water turns into ice, it all turns into ice together."

The time is out of joint. Perhaps the Time Wars have been lost and we are now, as Argüelles's Mayan prophecy warns, heading toward biospheric collapse. Perhaps, though, there is still time; and perhaps the number 13 is one of the keys to it all. Perhaps living on a 13:20 frequency (thirteen months of twenty-eight days apiece in thirteen-day cycles, with one annual "day out of time"—July 25—celebrated as a kind of universal sabbath or, as Argüelles puts it, "a Saturday night that just won't quit") might be worth trying out.

On March 27, 1995, José and Lloydine Argüelles appeared at the aptly named Babylon Restaurant in San Francisco to call on people to "change your calendars and enter the new time." During his talk, Argüelles remarked, "People say all the time, well, how can changing a calendar change anything? You have to understand, time is of the mind. The calendar you use is a measure of the mind. . . . Within three years of adopting the thirteen-moon calendar, we will see the end of money. Telepathy will be restored to us, and telepathy is God's natural government, the fourth-dimensional form of government. We are the only species right now that would rather watch television than practice telepathy. To live in cycles of time is to live in cosmic freedom."

At the conclusion of his speech, Argüelles motioned to his wife and said, "We live by trust. People think we are crazy. And we are. We are good crazy. Thirteen-twenty crazy." As he displayed a copy of a thirteen-moon calendar—one of many that he and his friends have been designing and printing up during the past few years—Lloydine, standing by a nearby table and holding up a traditional Gregorian calendar, lit a match; and the document representing the doomed, materialistic 12:60 world went up in flames, its ashes falling into a large metal bowl.

A Tale of the Thirteenth Floor

by Ogden Nash

The hands of the clock were reaching high
In an old midtown hotel;
I name no name, but its sordid fame
Is table talk in hell.
I name no name, but hell's own flame
Illumes the lobby garish,
A gilded snare just off Times Square
For the maidens of the parish.

The revolving door swept the grimy floor
Like a crinoline grotesque,
And a lowly bum from an ancient slum
Crept furtively past the desk.
His footsteps sift into the lift
As a knife in the sheath is slipped,
Stealthy and swift into the lift
As a vampire into a crypt.

Old Maxie, the elevator boy,
Was reading an ode by Shelley,
But he dropped the ode as it were a toad
When the gun jammed into his belly.
There came a whisper as soft as mud
In the bed of an old canal:
"Take me up to the suite of Pinball Pete,
The rat who betrayed my gal."

The lift doth rise with groans and sighs
Like a duchess for the waltz,
Then in middle shaft, like a duchess daft,
It changes its mind and halts.
The bum bites lip as the landlocked ship
Doth neither fall nor rise,
But Maxie the elevator boy
Regards him with burning eyes.
"First, to explore the thirteenth floor,"
Says Maxie, "would be wise."

Quoth the bum, "There is moss on your double cross,
I have been this way before,
I have cased the joint at every point,
And there is no thirteenth floor.
The architect he skipped direct
From twelve unto fourteen,
There is twelve below and fourteen above,
And nothing in between,
For the vermin who dwell in this hotel
Could never abide thirteen."

Said Max, "Thirteen, that floor obscene,
Is hidden from human sight;
But once a year it doth appear,
On this Walpurgis Night.
Ere you peril your soul in murderer's role,
Heed those who sinned of yore;
The path they trod led away from God,

And onto the thirteenth floor,
Where those they slew, a grisly crew,
Reproach them forevermore.

"We are higher than twelve and below fourteen,"
Said Maxie to the bum,
"And the sickening draft that taints the shaft
Is a whiff of kingdom come.
The sickening draft that taints the shaft
Blows through the devil's door!"
And he squashed the latch like a fungus patch,
And revealed the thirteenth floor.

It was cheap cigars like lurid scars
That glowed in the rancid gloom,
The murk was a-boil with fusel oil
And the reek of stale perfume.
And round and round there dragged and wound
A loathsome conga chain,
The square and the hep in slow lock step,
The slayer and the slain.
(For the souls of the victims ascend on high,
But their bodies below remain.)

The clean souls fly to their home in the sky,
But their bodies remain below
To pursue the Cain who each has slain
And harry him to and fro.
When life is extinct each corpse is linked

To its gibbering murderer,
As a chicken is bound with wire around
The neck of a killer cur.

Handcuffed to Hate come Doctor Waite
(He tastes the poison now),
And Ruth and Judd and a head of blood
With horns upon its brow.
Up sashays Nan with her feathery fan
From Floradora bright;
She never hung for Caesar Young,
But she's dancing with him tonight.

Here's the bulging hip and the foam-flecked lip
Of the mad dog, Vincent Coll,
And over there that ill-met pair,
Becker and Rosenthal.
Here's Legs and Dutch and a dozen such
Of braggart bullies and brutes,
And each one bends 'neath the weight of friends
Who are wearing concrete suits.

Now the damned make way for the double-damned
Who emerge with shuffling pace
From the nightmare zone of persons unknown,
With neither name nor face.
And poor Dot King to one doth cling,
Joined in a ghastly jig,

While Elwell doth jape at a goblin shape
And tickle it with his wig.

See Rothstein pass like breath on a glass,
The original Black Sox kid;
He riffles the pack, riding piggyback
On the killer whose name he hid.
And smeared like brine on a slavering swine,
Starr Faithful, once so fair,
Drawn from the sea to her debauchee,
With the salt sand in her hair.

And still they come, and from the bum
The icy sweat doth spray;
His white lips scream as in a dream,
"For God's sake, let's away!
If ever I meet with Pinball Pete
I will not seek his gore,
Lest a treadmill grim I must trudge with him
On the hideous thirteenth floor."

"For you I rejoice," said Maxie's voice,
"And I bid you go in peace,
But I am late for a dancing date
That nevermore will cease.
So remember, friend, as your way you wend,
That it would have happened to you,
But I turned the heat on Pinball Pete;
You see—I had a daughter, too!"

The bum reached out and he tried to shout,
But the door in his face was slammed,
And silent as stone he rode down alone
From the floor of the double-damned.